THE
FREEDOM
CONVOY

THE FREEDOM CONVOY

The Inside Story of Three Weeks
that Shook the World

by
Andrew Lawton

SUTHERLAND
HOUSE

TORONTO, 2022

Sutherland House
416 Moore Ave., Suite 205
Toronto, ON M4G 1C9

First edition, June 2022

If you are interested in inviting one of our authors to a live event or
media appearance, please contact sranasinghe@sutherlandhousebooks.com
and visit our website at sutherlandhousebooks.com for more
information about our authors and their schedules.

Manufactured in Canada
Cover designed by Jordan Lunn
Book composed by Karl Hunt

Library and Archives Canada Cataloguing in Publication
Title: The Freedom Convoy : the inside story of three weeks
that shook the world / Andrew Lawton.
Names: Lawton, Andrew, author.
Identifiers: Canadiana 20220245223 | ISBN 9781989555934 (softcover)
Subjects: LCSH: Protest movements—Canada. |
LCSH: Truck drivers—Canada. | LCSH: Vaccine mandates—
Canada. | LCSH: Liberty.
Classification: LCC HM883 .L39 2022 |
DDC 303.48/40971—dc23

ISBN 978-1-989555-93-4

For my infinitely loving and supportive wife,
Jennifer, and my parents, Jim and Trish.

CONTENTS

INTRODUCTION

On the eve of the convoy's arrival in Ottawa, the streets felt more like a party than a protest. Honks, diesel exhaust, and excitement filled the air. Drivers rounded city blocks blaring their horns, blasting music, and shouting "Freedom!" as they passed cheering gaggles on the sidewalks. The early arrivals—truckers who showed up on their own rather than in the several convoys set to descend on Canada's capital—staked positions on Wellington St. and its immediate side streets. Many of them wouldn't leave those spots for three weeks. The scene indoors was just as vibrant. People who only knew each other from Facebook and Telegram groups met for the first time and embraced. Hotels that had sat empty for much of the previous two years filled up.

In the days that followed, the atmosphere would become even more festive. A flatbed truck rigged with a high-powered sound system became the main stage, hosting speakers and musicians throughout the week. People sang and danced into the night. The same stage hosted church services on Sunday mornings. And then there were the bouncy castles and the hot tub. Walking into Convoyland felt like taking a step into 2019—a time before mask mandates and vaccine passports. This is the world the protesters were trying to reclaim. If you were there, you'd never know the participants were supposed to be a bunch of violent, hateful insurrectionists. Contrary to what you've been told, they weren't.

As the truckers neared Ottawa, Prime Minister Justin Trudeau dismissed them as a "small fringe minority" with "unacceptable views."[1] Canadian media coverage oscillated between dismissive and slanderous. One outlet highlighted a purported security expert's warning that convoy donors might be financing terrorism.[2] Canada's state broadcaster, CBC, mused that "Russian actors" might be behind everything.[3] When the convoy established its semi-permanent presence in Ottawa—which one organizer dubbed "Trudeau's Truck Stop"—the stories that trended on Twitter and dominated mainstream media coverage were almost universally negative. Stealing food from the homeless, desecrating monuments, Nazi and Confederate flags, and so on. Most of these incidents were wildly misrepresented. The convoy's organizers were swift to condemn bad actors in their midst, and none of them were representative of the protesters as a whole. Nonetheless, these stories helped critics craft a narrative that the convoy was made up of a bunch of lawless, callous white supremacists.

These controversies generated far more buzz online than they did on the streets of Ottawa. Generally, I only learned of them when I was back in my hotel room warming up and recharging my phone. I didn't see a single swastika or Confederate battle flag in my travels, although from the news coverage you'd think they were everywhere. There were lots of 'Fuck Trudeau' flags and no shortage of signs delving into any number of conspiracy theories involving 5G, George Soros, and Bill Gates, but sprinklings of incivility and kookiness are not violence.

The divide between the media's portrayal of the convoy and the reality on the ground was stark. Even though the mainstream Canadian coverage occurred at close range—the action was all unfolding steps from Ottawa news bureaus—reporters and columnists insisted the truckers and their supporters were dangerous goons. American and British outlets gave the convoy a fairer treatment. Some of this was no doubt exacerbated by convoy organizers' refusal to engage with most media outlets, and the tendency of some protesters to heckle or harass journalists they encountered, resulting in unflattering news clips that further maligned the convoy. People who saw for themselves what the convoy was like grew more distrustful of the media's coverage of it. Some of my most-praised coverage was simple live video streaming, showing viewers the unfiltered reality of life in what Ottawa police called the 'red zone.'

Few journalists sought to understand the protesters and why they were there. Whether it was the HVAC technician who showed up to check things out for a weekend and never left, the fully vaccinated lefty who protested because she felt being pro-choice required opposing vaccine mandates, or the Alberta couple who walked into a hotel looking for a printer and ended up becoming a critical part of one of the convoy's logistics hubs, there was room for everyone in the convoy. Over the three weeks, the convoy attracted a broad base of support, including from people who didn't fit the moulds into which their critics sought to shove them. There were evangelicals and libertarians, Indigenous Canadians and Québécois, hippies and blue-collar workers. The convoy was far more reflective of Canadian society than many would assume. This diversity was why efforts to castigate all the protesters as knuckle-dragging, anti-science louts were misguided. Yet for all their differences, there was something that held the protesters together. It started with shared opposition to vaccine mandates and vaccine passports and morphed into a sense of community for people who otherwise felt like social and political outcasts. That bond kept the convoy together until the end, when two days of aggressive police action cleared the streets, removing the trucks and protesters in under forty-eight hours.

On that cold February weekend, mounted police knocked an elderly Indigenous woman to the ground, cops in riot gear pepper-sprayed journalists, the government conscripted tow truck drivers, and banks froze hundreds of accounts of people who'd never been accused, let alone convicted, of any crimes. That weekend ushered in the beginning of the end of the convoy's time in Ottawa. It was also the first and only violent turn in the otherwise peaceful protest. This crackdown was largely celebrated by the Canadian media and condemned by foreign press. To the convoy's supporters, it was proof of the very government overreach they were protesting; to the convoy's detractors, it was long overdue. This clash only furthered the divide between the two narratives.

At the end of the day, the convoy did manage to spark a political reckoning, albeit mostly within the Conservative Party of Canada. It also revealed the disconnect between the media and those it covers. More importantly, it signalled a turning point in Canadian politics and in Canada's pandemic.

This book is the product of my on-the-ground reporting in Ottawa and countless hours of interviews with those involved in the convoy at various levels. It does not purport to be the definitive account of everything that happened in those three weeks. There are elements of the story I have not addressed at length: the arguments for and against vaccines and vaccine mandates; what was happening inside police forces faced with a giant, carnival-like protest; the experiences of Ottawa citizens whose streets were taken over by the protesters, to name just a few. These angles were well-covered by media as events unfolded, often at the expense of delving into how and why the convoy came to be. I've focused on this story because it is the one I most wanted to read. I was repeatedly struck in Ottawa by the divergence between media coverage of the convoy and what I saw with my own eyes. In part because they were not talking to mainstream media, protesters and organizers were often missing or even misrepresented in their own story. I wanted to understand their thoughts and motives, and write about the convoy as they experienced it. I have sought to do so here, accurately and honestly.

The convoy's story is a fascinating one. One about Canadians, who generally welcomed each wave of Covid restrictions, finally deciding they'd had enough, and in large numbers declaring the pandemic over. About a scrappy group of truckers bringing a G-7 capital to its knees. About an earnest, grassroots movement evolving into a multimillion-dollar operation with lawyers, accountants, a public relations strategy, back-channel police negotiations, and multiple command centres spread out across Ottawa hotels. And about a protest that spawned spinoffs and copycats, not just across Canada but around the world.

PART I

THE JOURNEY

CHAPTER 1

THE MAKINGS OF
A CONVOY

Brigitte Belton had crossed the Canada-United States border more times than she could count. On November 16, 2021, it was different. A run-in with an overzealous border guard would push her to the breaking point.

The 52-year-old trucker from Wallaceburg, Ontario, was driving into Canada with a load and no one else in the truck, just her dog. The Canada Border Services Agency officer at the Windsor-Detroit crossing threatened her with arrest. Her crime? Talking to the officer in the wicket without a mask. Belton wasn't trying to be obstinate. She's asthmatic and is a domestic violence survivor. She says having her face covered sends her "off into the deep end." Usually when she'd crossed the border, the agents were understanding. Sometimes she was allowed to wear a plastic face shield instead, which didn't cause her the same grief as a mask. This time, there was no such compassion.

Belton was sent into the secondary screening area and warned again that she could be arrested by Windsor police for not complying. After a conversation with a supervisor, she was released with a warning, but the experience rattled her. So much so that she nearly got into an accident—something she said had never happened in her seven years of driving truck. A couple of hours later, she pulled into the Husky truck stop near London, just off Highway 401, and recounted the incident in a teary TikTok video.

"In Canada, we're no longer free," Belton said in the video. "I'm done. I'm done. I don't know what I'm going to do next, but I'm done."[4]

It wasn't just about the border incident, but nearly two years of lockdowns, restrictions, and mandates that made Belton, who never got vaccinated against COVID-19, feel like a second-class citizen in her own country. She thought of ending her life. She even tried to move her bank accounts to her husband's name, but this plan was thwarted when she learned she had to go into a bank branch in person during business hours to do it. In the meantime, people who saw her video reached out to console her. Belton also spoke with her husband, who was able to calm her down.

Since September, the unvaccinated were barred from going to restaurants, gyms and most recreational venues in Ontario. All provinces ended up imposing vaccine passport regimes, even the conservative holdouts of Alberta and Saskatchewan. In October, Prime Minister Justin Trudeau implemented a sweeping vaccine mandate for air and rail travel, as well as for federal public servants. By the time of Belton's run-in with the CBSA officer, her truck felt like her only respite from a world that was closing off to her.

"At that point I was done," she told me. "I was done with life. I knew I couldn't live in Canada in an open-air jail. I just couldn't."

Little did Belton know, things were about to get worse.

On November 19, two days after Belton's mask altercation, the Canadian government imposed a *de facto* vaccine mandate for cross-border truckers.[5] Belton was about to lose her livelihood.

Truckers kept crossing the Canada-United States border when it was first closed in March 2020 at the start of the COVID-19 pandemic As essential workers, they were exempt from Canada's numerous COVID requirements, including PCR testing, quarantine, and, later on, the need to show proof of vaccination. The exemption was uncontroversial. Truckers are critical to Canadian and American supply chains and pose a low public health risk as people who work in relative isolation. When the Canadian border reopened to vaccinated American travellers on August 9, 2021, unvaccinated truckers continued to enter without quarantine and without issue.

The November 19 announcement eliminated the essential worker exemption, effective January 15, 2022. This meant unvaccinated American truckers would be barred from Canada, and unvaccinated Canadian truckers would have to quarantine upon re-entry, making it impractical to continue hauling. Days later, US President Joe Biden followed suit, announcing Canadian truckers would have to be vaccinated to enter the United States as of January 22.[6]

Trudeau's vaccine mandate for truckers looked far more like scorn than science. At the time, Canada had among the highest vaccination rates in the world, with over 86 percent of adults fully vaccinated.[7] Why now? Countries around the world were lifting their restrictions. Many American states had completely reopened, and those that hadn't were quickly doing so. Yet Canada was adding more restrictions and barriers, especially to the unvaccinated.

The move was condemned by trucking industry groups on both sides of the border. Canadian Trucking Alliance (CTA) president Stephen Laskowski warned the mandate would create a "perfect storm," exacerbating existing supply chain disruptions and delays.[8]

At the time there were already 18,000 trucking job vacancies in Canada, and empty grocery store shelves were becoming a regular sight for Canadians. According to the CTA, there were 120,000 Canadian and 40,000 American cross-border truckers. Of those, the CTA "conservatively" estimated 10 to 20 percent of the Canadian truckers and 40 percent of the American truckers would be cut out of cross-border trade because of Biden's and Trudeau's vaccine mandates. Belton was one of them.

She was skeptical of getting a "chemical shot up my arm from some type of pharmaceutical company," she said.[9] Mandates only bolstered her aversion to the vaccine, because she felt if the vaccine was as safe and effective as governments said, they wouldn't need to force people to take it.

"I am going to lose my job," she told me. "I've got a truck that I stupidly bought during a pandemic because I was an essential worker. I didn't think they'd ever take me off the road. If I can be essential for two years, how come I'm not essential now? Was it all a lie then? Or is it all a lie now?"

Trudeau had long abandoned his idealization of essential workers, at least those who weren't double jabbed. Canadians had, too, it seemed. In September 2021, Trudeau won re-election after a campaign during which he regularly took aim at the unvaccinated in rhetoric and policy. He pledged to make vaccination a prerequisite to work in the federal public sector or travel by air or rail. He made good on this just a few weeks after the election.

* * *

The vaccine mandate for truckers didn't add to Belton's despair, oddly. Instead of giving up on Canada, she had an idea. In her TikTok scrolling, she had come across another Canadian trucker who, like her, had clearly had enough of the COVID era—BigRed1975.

In real life, BigRed is Chris Barber, a Saskatchewan trucker and prolific TikTok influencer with a large following. Belton had never met him, but liked the way he discussed COVID restrictions and felt they were on the same wavelength politically. Like her, she thought he was at his breaking point. On one of his videos about the trucker vaccine mandate, she left a comment with a simple message: "Convoy 2022." When he didn't respond, she posted about the idea of doing a convoy on another video. And another. And another. ("I'm kind of a pushy little girl," she admitted). She kept going until she got his attention, then convinced him to talk on the phone so she could pitch her idea.

"Let's just get a group of people together. We'll drive around, we'll make some noise, we'll do some slow rolls, and honestly, this is going to be solved in 24 hours," Belton said to Barber in early December.

Belton's vision was to have simultaneous trucker convoys in cities and at border crossings across Canada tying up traffic so no one could look away. Another idea was a national trucker work stoppage, though she and Barber both preferred the convoy. Naively, she thought the government would cave in less than a day. After planting the seed with Barber, she kept nudging him along, putting her network marketing background to use persuading him to use his contacts and audience to help make it happen. She convinced him, and the Convoy to End Mandates—as it was then called—was born.

Interest in the convoy spread quickly across TikTok and Facebook. There was a momentary victory when Canada Border Services Agency said on January 12—three days before the trucker mandate was supposed to go into effect—it would continue allowing unvaccinated American and Canadian truckers into the country as it had before.[10] Those gearing up for the convoy thought Trudeau was already buckling, although the victory was short-lived. The government reversed course the next afternoon, saying truckers would still have to be vaccinated effective January 15, dismissing the earlier about face as an "error" from the CBSA.[11] Even in the brief period when they thought the mandate was gone, Barber and Belton forged ahead with their convoy planning, knowing that their cause was much larger than just the trucker mandate.

"It's not just for us," Belton said in a January 15 video. "It's for EMS. It's for police. It's for fire. It's for moms. It's for dads. It's for everyone."[12]

Belton whipped up a flyer to share the details on social media, and soon after others joined to lead convoys in different regions. She was going to spearhead a Sarnia segment while Barber rallied trucks in Saskatchewan. Other regional leaders stepped forward in Calgary, Winnipeg, and Windsor early on, too. The wheels were in motion, so to speak.

* * *

On August 29, 2021, a few dozen truckers blocked a highway on Australia's Gold Coast for several hours to protest mandatory vaccination for essential workers.[13] Afterwards, they set their sights on the capital of Canberra in New South Wales. Alberta activist James

Bauder saw this and envisioned a Canadian version. He put out a call on Facebook for 500 trucks to drive to Ottawa with him seeking an end to vaccine passports, mask mandates, and lockdowns.

"If you have a Semi Truck and are willing to Step Up to save our Great Nation from becoming Chinada text me," he wrote. "I am ready to make some noise but I need you Big Trucker."[14]

The idea had been tried before. In February 2019, 170 trucks left Red Deer, Alberta in a convoy to Ottawa protesting the Trudeau government's energy policies. The drivers and other demonstrators held two days of rallies in Ottawa, attracting fairly mainstream conservative support, including a speech by then-Conservative Party of Canada leader Andrew Scheer. A GoFundMe campaign for United We Roll raised $142,873. Organizers trumpeted their success and everyone returned home without issue.[15]

Bauder was there for United We Roll, and thought COVID would make an even better backdrop. During the pandemic, he founded Canada Unity, a purportedly "humanitarian" Facebook page and online network which posts anti-vaccine mandate and anti-vaccine content. A December 30, 2021 post called vaccine-related injuries a "genocide" and suggested it was unsafe to travel on a plane flown by a vaccinated pilot.[16] One of Canada Unity's campaigns was collecting signatures for a so-called memorandum of understanding (MOU), a six-page document bizarrely directed at the Canadian Senate and Governor General Mary Simon. The MOU claims to create a "Citizens of Canada Committee" between signatories, senators, and the Queen's representative in Canada, which would be empowered to order provincial, municipal and federal governments to drop vaccine mandates and vaccine passports. The MOU is nonsense couched in legalese, but this can be convincing for those who don't know better, especially given the confidence (and relentlessness) with which Bauder has promoted it.

Over the fall of 2021, Bauder ginned up support for his convoy idea and the MOU, and in December drove from Alberta to Ottawa in "Unity 1," a camper decked out in Canada Unity insignia, to deliver the MOU to the Senate of Canada in person, a mission he dubbed Operation Bearhug. He only found one 18-wheeler willing to go to Ottawa—a far cry from the 500 he asked for—but he was able to assemble dozens of protesters when he got there. Bauder led a protest group to the Senate building where parliamentary precinct security guards told him they couldn't accept any documents on site. Bauder improvised and led his group to a nearby Canada Post outlet, where he paid—unnecessarily, as letters to parliament and the Governor General don't require postage—to send the MOU by registered mail. Bauder returned home, and Canada Unity promised "big developments" in 2022.

Belton had never heard of Bauder, Canada Unity, or the memorandum of understanding. As word travelled about the Convoy to End Mandates, Bauder contacted Belton through a women-in-trucking group and offered to join forces. On a call in early January, Bauder sold Barber and Belton on the idea of going to Ottawa instead of arranging simultaneous regional convoys. He thought the key to ending Covid restrictions and vaccine mandates was public pressure at the federal level. To promote the idea, Bauder looped in Pat King, a self-proclaimed "investigative journalist" with hundreds of thousands of Facebook followers. King announced the plan for an Ottawa convoy in a January 12 Facebook video.[17]

The next evening, King hosted a 71-minute Facebook live stream with Belton, Barber, Bauder and two of the fledgling convoy's regional organizers, Dale Enns and Joe Janzen.[18] At one point, 3,000 people tuned in. It was apparent during the discussion that Bauder had taken it upon himself to adopt a key planning role. He promoted his memorandum of understanding during the stream. He also shared— to Belton's surprise—that a third convoy route had been added from the Maritimes through Quebec, in addition to the Vancouver-Ottawa and Sarnia-Ottawa routes. He spoke about the importance of a day-by-day itinerary accounting for food, fuel, and lodging requirements. The west-to-east convoy would follow the United We Roll route from 2019. The plan was to flesh out the itinerary in the coming days, then post it to Canada Unity's website as a central reference point, which would also provide contact information for the various regional road captains. During the discussions, the venture also took on a new name: the Convoy to End Mandates became Freedom Convoy 2022.

CHAPTER 2

FROM MOVEMENT TO ORGANIZATION

Brigitte Belton's idea of a national series of trucker slow rolls had coalesced with James Bauder's vision of a convoy to Ottawa. Bauder took the lead in putting the itineraries together, with a planned arrival date of January 29. Belton pushed for January 28, the anniversary of the *Challenger* explosion. She was convinced there was a parallel between the explosion and governments' pandemic response measures.

"That was the day the shuttle blew up," Belton told me. "That was science. Science is only as good as the data it's given."

Belton eventually led a group to Ottawa on January 28 regardless, which was one of several sources of frustration with her from other organizers.

Conservative corners of the internet were buzzing with news of the convoy by the middle of January, although plans were still in flux. The convoy didn't have a website or a social media presence apart from the personal channels of people promoting it. Belton and Chris Barber fielded messages all day long from people who wanted to get involved. They were planning from the road, pulling over to post TikTok updates and respond to the endless stream of questions and comments. Most were just words of encouragement, but others asked when the convoys were leaving, where they were meeting, and, increasingly, how they could financially support the project.

Neither Barber nor Belton had previously thought of money. Both were planning to pay their own way to Ottawa and assumed others would do the same. They were just excited a growing number of their fellow truckers and "four wheelers"—car and pickup drivers— wanted to do the same. That changed on January 13, when Barber got a call from Tamara Lich.

Lich was born Arlene Catherine Martineau on September 19, 1972 in rural Saskatchewan. She was given the name Tamara by her adoptive parents. Lich was an established activist in Medicine Hat, a southern Alberta city of 63,000. In 2018 and 2019, she spearheaded local yellow vest protests, a conservative movement that took its inspiration from protests in France for economic justice. She was also on the board of the Maverick Party, an upstart western independence party which had run a slate of candidates in the 2021 federal election. In 2019, Lich was a supporter of the United We Roll convoy, but didn't follow it to Ottawa. Apart from a family trip there when she was five years old, Lich had never been to the capital. Independent of Bauder, Barber, and Belton, Lich had thought Canada might be ripe for another convoy, so she immediately wanted in when she learned of their efforts.

Lich contacted Barber through a mutual acquaintance and offered to manage a crowdfunding campaign and social media page for the convoy, which at this point was being promoted by lots of people, but had no central hub for information. Barber and Belton were having trouble keeping up, especially while spending their days driving truck, so accepting the offer was a no-brainer. On January 14, Lich created the Freedom Convoy 2022 Facebook page and a GoFundMe campaign.

"We are asking for donations to help with the costs of fuel, food, and lodgings to help ease the pressures of this arduous task," the campaign's fundraising pitch read. "It's a small price to pay for our freedoms. We thank you all for your donations and know that you are helping reshape this once beautiful country back to the way it was."

Lich expected to raise $20,000 to buy some diesel and sandwiches for the truckers. She laughed at Barber when he suggested setting the fundraising target at $250,000.

"Oh my God, I am not doing that," she told him. "That sounds greedy. No way am I doing that. I'm going to set it for $100,000, and I still feel bad about that."

The campaign hit six figures in just two days.

With donations ranging from a few dollars to thousands of dollars, the GoFundMe brought in hundreds of thousands of dollars in its first few days. Within a week, it reached $1 million, and the trucks hadn't even hit the road. There was no plan for that amount of money, let alone what came next.

Because Lich's name was on the GoFundMe and she was posting regular video updates on the Freedom Convoy 2022 Facebook page, she quickly became the most visible leader of this grassroots movement. The money was the most tangible way of measuring the convoy's momentum, although the campaign's growth invited questions about how that sum was going to be spent. The plan was always to give it directly to truckers to pay for fuel first, then food and lodging if necessary. Any leftover funds would be donated to a veterans' organization. Lich updated the GoFundMe description to explain that she would disburse the money through e-transfers, prompting a registration drive so organizers knew which truckers were participating.

Lich was not prepared to handle tens of thousands of dollars, let alone the millions the campaign eventually raised. Beyond the GoFundMe campaign, people also sent e-transfers, which went into a dedicated personal account in Lich's name. Even though the convoy was still not on the road, things were moving quickly. Lich assembled a finance committee comprised of accountants, bookkeepers, a First Nations financial liaison, a few directors, and herself to oversee the distribution of donations. At the outset, organizers assumed drivers would pay their own way and save their receipts to be reimbursed later. However, Lich didn't want to exclude those of lesser means, especially when it came to truckers who were out of work because of the very mandates they were joining the convoy to protest. One solution was to advance cash to those who needed it, although with only days to go until the rollout, the bureaucratic process to get money out of the GoFundMe campaign made this impossible. Initially, Lich praised GoFundMe for being great to work with as she and the platform sorted out a plan to release the money. One proposal from GoFundMe, Lich said, was to transfer money directly to a bulk fuel company and let it handle fuelling the trucks. This was a relief to Lich, who did not want to deal with all the e-transfers and receipts, or give anyone an opportunity to accuse organizers of pocketing money. The organizers weren't even looking to be reimbursed for their own travel expenses.

As the convoy gained steam online, other people unconnected with the central organizing team started creating their own online fundraising campaigns, ostensibly to support the truckers. Some wanted to pay for hotels or to buy them food. Others set up campaigns to crowdfund their own journeys to Ottawa to join the convoy. Some campaigns looked like the work of scammers trying to cash in on the generosity of those supporting the truckers. Lich never discouraged people from donating to alternate campaigns, but asked supporters in several videos to do their "due diligence" and stressed that her campaign was the only 'official' one.

* * *

Shortly after getting involved, Lich thought the convoy needed to come up with a public relations plan. She was communicating details about the convoy and its fundraising on social media, but that wasn't enough. She was worried the truckers might not be the best spokespeople for the protest, at least not without media training. She also didn't trust that the media would accurately characterize those who did speak up, making it all the more important to have someone who knew what to look out for. She asked long-time conservative activist and organizer Benjamin Dichter to come aboard as spokesperson. Lich met Dichter in 2018 in Medicine Hat at a talk about radical Islam by Tom Quiggin, an author and former security analyst whose podcast Dichter produced. Dichter was a Conservative Party of Canada candidate in an unwinnable Toronto riding in the 2015 election. He was also a co-founder of the LGBT Conservative organization LGBTory (although he's not LGBT). Lich kept in touch with Dichter over the years, but didn't know he had started trucking part-time shortly before the COVID pandemic. Not only did he understand the media, he was also a trucker.

Like Barber, Dichter was fully vaccinated. But he was firmly against vaccine mandates and COVID restrictions, and saw growing opposition to them from Canadians as a whole. He was happy to get involved, but he had two conditions: the convoy had to remain in Ottawa, and political parties had to be kept out of the protest. He knew some politicians would be supportive, but he wanted to avoid the movement being branded with any specific partisan colors. He thought the convoy needed to stay in Ottawa because he didn't want it to be a flash in the pan that didn't translate to any substantive change.

Things were moving so quickly, Dichter didn't have long to put together a media strategy, but the message was a simple one. "We're here just to end the mandates, and then the vaccine passports. Nothing more," he told me. He couldn't prevent others with ulterior motives or kookier tactics from speaking, but he and the organizers would be clear that those people didn't speak for the convoy.

The immediate problems were Bauder and Pat King. Despite Bauder's assistance with developing the itineraries, other organizers grew wary of his involvement, especially his relentless use of the convoy to promote his memorandum of understanding. King promoted the convoy in live streams to his 300,000 followers on Facebook, where he also peddled conspiracy theories like challenging the Holocaust's death toll. In a widely circulated clip from a December 2021 stream, King mused about violent revolution and suggested COVID restrictions would only end "with bullets." King argued the comment was taken out of context.[19] In another video, King said someone is going to make Prime Minister Justin Trudeau "catch a bullet one day," which King later claimed was just a prediction, not an endorsement. King's aggressive tone and unrestrained tongue posed a problem to a movement rallying in support of a peaceful protest.

Dichter hadn't heard of King or Bauder until the convoy was en route to Ottawa and he started getting questions about the memorandum of understanding. King was never an organizer (though he was undoubtedly an early booster) and Bauder had been kept out of the loop of a lot of discussions by other organizers. Neither had any involvement with the fundraising, but Dichter saw them both as liabilities and urged the group to cut any remaining ties to them.

Lich and Barber tried to pre-empt some criticism by putting out the call to the media and would-be rabble rousers that the convoy was a peaceful, lawful demonstration. In a January 20 TikTok video, Barber said that anybody who breaks "the rules" of the convoy was out. Those rules included giving emergency vehicles the right of way, respecting law enforcement, and remaining peaceful.[20]

"Right now, the public is 100 percent on the truckers' and . . . the removal of the mandates' side. We don't want to lose that. When we start acting like assholes, we lose that."

Lich went further in a live Facebook video on January 23, asking convoy participants to tell organizers about any illegal, violent, or hateful behaviour so they could forward it to police, asserting "that is not us."[21]

Despite the convoy's clear message and disavowal of people like King, Dichter felt they couldn't rely on mainstream media to represent the protest, the protesters, or even the cause accurately. But he didn't want to spend all his time on defense.

"The plan was to attack them," Dichter said of the mainstream media. "To kind of out them for what they are. One stage was to ignore them, but it was to basically raise them up on a pedestal and cut their heads off in front of everybody and make everybody see what has happened to legacy media that's entirely scripted, bought and paid for."

Skepticism and, at times, outright contempt from conservatives toward the mainstream media has been growing for several years, especially since the Trudeau government unleashed a range of subsidy programs for news organizations. Dichter and most convoy supporters thought the media were so hellbent on carrying water for Trudeau that the truckers would never get a fair hearing.

Dichter decided early on he wouldn't engage with outlets he thought were not approaching the convoy in good faith. He did plenty of interviews, but they were almost exclusively with independent journalists or filmmakers, except for a few conservative-leaning television networks like Fox News and Newsmax in the United States and GB News in the United Kingdom. This strategy meant misinformation would sometimes fester in the media because Dichter and other spokespeople didn't bother to correct the record.

"Once I respond, I'm stepping into their narrative and I'm stepping into their filter," Dichter said. "Their narrative and filter is BS and it should be mocked and disregarded from the onset. I'm not going to step into theirs; they're going to step into ours. (That was) my approach to it."

Dichter appeared on the Fox News show *Tucker Carlson Tonight* on Thursday, January 27, in a brief interview that not only put on record to an international audience the convoy's opposition to vaccine mandates and passports, but also set off what would become an ongoing fascination with the convoy among the American right.[22]

CHAPTER 3

ON TO OTTAWA

The first leg of the Freedom Convoy rolled out from a truck stop in Delta, British Columbia, before dawn on Sunday, January 23, beginning the six-day journey to Ottawa. Another convoy set out shortly after from Prince George, BC. The official itinerary had the main western convoy overnighting in Calgary, Regina, Thunder Bay, Sault Ste. Marie, then finally Arnprior just outside of Ottawa, before arriving on Parliament Hill on Saturday, January 29. Throughout the week, smaller groups were scheduled to meet up with the main convoy. Other routes from Atlantic Canada, southern Ontario, and Quebec would depart as the week progressed. The original grand vision was for all the trucks from all over the country to show up in Ottawa on the same day.

The GoFundMe campaign cleared $1.5 million by the morning of January 23, yet despite ongoing discussions between Tamara Lich and the crowdfunding company, none of the money had been released. Truckers and organizers dipped into their own pockets and spotted others who were having trouble with fuel costs. Generally, each province had two road captains who were responsible for registering the truckers in the convoy. Some road captains were more organized than others. The position came out of the finance committee's attempt to find a way to identity who was in the convoy to know who to reimburse with donations. While good in theory, the plan devolved into varying degrees of chaos as scads of unregistered vehicles showed up. Dale Enns, one of two road captains for Manitoba, was responsible for a group of about 100 truckers who registered to join the convoy. Enns, a cross-border trucker himself, set out on Wednesday from Brandon. Like other road captains, he quickly saw there were far more vehicles on the road than in his registry. While Enns personally fronted some truckers for money because of the GoFundMe delays, he said most drivers weren't all that concerned with the money. They just wanted to be involved.

At the Delta rollout, supporters cheered on the truckers from overpasses, waving Canadian flags and holding signs with messages like "Thank you truckers!" and "Truck Trudeau" (and one saying "Covid-19 Vaccine Not Safe!!!"). All the drivers I spoke to said how memorable and moving the sight was. As one remarked, it was humbling to see ordinary Canadians cheering you on after the government has said you don't deserve to keep your job because you're not vaccinated. The sights on Delta overpasses were not outliers. In Salmon Arm, BC, a city of less than 18,000 east of Kamloops, dozens of cars were parked on the shoulders as supporters waved the convoy through town with flags and signs. This was the norm at every point of the journey: overpasses, shoulders, and even random fields along the Trans-Canada Highway were filled with people who wanted the truckers to know they had their backs—even in frigid January prairie weather. Hundreds of supporters turned out in Chris Barber's Saskatchewan hometown of Swift Current when the convoy rolled through. Originally, Barber planned to mount an upside-down Canadian flag on his truck, the signal for a nation in distress.

When he saw the outpouring, he made sure to put the flag right side up, because he was inspired by what looked like a country and its citizens turning a corner. Lich was constantly in disbelief. "I'm going to cry all the way to Ottawa, I swear to God," she said in one of her Facebook videos. It was a common theme. Lich said she was never a crier until the convoy, when the outpouring of support overwhelmed her at every turn.

On Monday morning, Lich met Barber in-person for the first time in a truck stop parking lot in Medicine Hat. Barber lives on a farm in Swift Current, where he runs his own trucking company. He had just returned to Saskatchewan after hauling a load, then headed west to meet the convoy in Calgary, which was the first overnight stop. Barber led the convoy for most of the journey, but Lich's parents had the honour of setting the pace on the way out of Medicine Hat. Lich rode shotgun with Barber so they could continue their planning with each other, the road captains, and the arrival team in Ottawa. Lich wasn't worried about five days in a truck with a stranger because, to her, Barber wasn't a stranger. They felt like lifelong friends. They had been speaking by phone at all hours for at least ten days and formed an instant bond. In any event, between Barber's regular communication over the CB radio, Lich's relentless Facebook live streams, a handful of media interviews and planning calls with other organizers, Lich and Barber didn't actually have that much time to talk to each other.

Most of the truckers spoke over CB, but another channel of communication opened up on Zello, a walkie-talkie phone app that connects users by the internet rather than radio frequency. With Zello, people could keep in touch from anywhere in the country or the world. Zello channels were crowded by convoy participants and supporters alike, and the occasional trolls (especially by the time the convoy arrived in Ottawa). At one point, the app got a Canadian celebrity cameo—country singer Paul Brandt, whose famous cover song "Convoy" had, for obvious reasons, become the Freedom Convoy's unofficial anthem.

"Truckers, I wear a hat and sing for a living. Canadian country singer Paul Brandt here," he said. "I've been listening with my wife and two kids and we want to say thank you for all you're doing in defence of civil liberties and freedom. You're inspiring the world and we stand with you."

Organizers told truck and car drivers to obey the rules of the road, and respect law enforcement. Barber, the road captains, and police regularly spoke with each other throughout the week. Several organizers told me police officers were privately offering their support for the convoy and its goals. At some parts of the drive, police gave the convoy escorts. At other points, they held back traffic at cross streets to let the convoy pass through uninterrupted.

* * *

While the journey to Ottawa was encouraging and memorable for the convoy's organizers, this positivity didn't stop cracks from forming in the team. Convoy supporters and critics alike questioned Lich and Dichter about Bauder's memorandum of understanding, a document filled with legal gobbledygook, which purports to have the power to trigger the dissolution of Justin Trudeau's government if enough people sign it and send it to the Senate and Canada's Governor General. Bauder and Brigitte Belton clashed for personal reasons. Belton claimed Bauder wanted to send a documentary crew to film her granddaughter's birth and fundraise off of it as a "gift from God" to the convoy. Belton stepped away from the leadership team, although she was eventually coaxed back after Bauder apologized. Bauder did not agree to be interviewed for this book and did not respond to emails requesting comment, but in a *Toronto Star* interview he said that he stepped away from the organizing committee over his dislike and distrust of Pat King.[23] This is disputed by other organizers who say Bauder's role was limited to helping devise the routes and publishing the maps on the Canada Unity website. King continued to promote the convoy as he followed it to Ottawa, to the chagrin of those trying to keep a unified and positive front.

"We tried to get rid of him," Dichter said of King. "I'm like 'Tamara, get rid of him. He's going to get you into trouble. He's going to get everybody into trouble. He doesn't use his brain. Get rid of him.'"

Lich's charm came in large part from her warmth. Everyone liked her, and she was in the business of making friends rather than enemies. Dichter, who was at home in Toronto as the western convoy headed east, was frustrated she wasn't as firm and decisive as her leadership role required, especially when it came to cutting people loose. For Lich's part, she was trying to build a movement, so turning people away was counterproductive, at least on the surface. She raised concerns with King at a couple of points in the journey, but he always had an explanation for everything. Eventually, she relented and told him to go home.

"You need to check your fucking ego, and if you care about this movement at all you will not go into Ottawa," Lich reportedly said to him in Sudbury on January 28.

According to two people with knowledge of the conversation, King broke down in tears. Organizers believed the problem was handled and King would return home to Alberta. Instead, he carried on as though he and Lich never spoke. Dichter drafted an official statement on King, asserting that he wasn't an organizer and spoke only for himself. Lich posted it to the Freedom Convoy Facebook page, but removed it the next day after backlash from King's supporters, who felt he was being unfairly thrown under the bus. Dichter said he was "a little bit pissed off," but understood the pressures. Lich ultimately re-posted another denunciation of King.

* * *

Just as the truckers were inspired by the supporters they saw on the roadside, many of those folks were inspired by the truckers. David Paisley, a duct worker from southern Ontario, heard rumblings about the convoy and wanted to see it for himself. Because of Belton's stubbornness about the date, the Ontario contingent split into two convoys, one heading to Ottawa on Thursday and the other on Friday. Paisley learned of the Thursday convoy heading east on the 401 through southern Ontario. When he got off work at noon, he looked on Google Maps and found a parking lot near an overpass in Guelph he thought would give him a good perch to see what it was all about. He didn't know what to expect, but realized this was something big the closer he got.

"I passed some other overpasses and I'm like 'Holy crap. This is a thing,'" he told me. "I pull into the parking lot, and there's a line-up of people. There are people handing out hot chocolate. There are flags everywhere. There are big banners, and families."

Like Paisley, the people he met just showed up. The Ontario convoys were generally the most disorganized, especially when it came to timing. No one knew when trucks would be passing through or how many there would be. Many of the well-wishers waited for hours. It was clear they were there to support the truckers and their protest against vaccine mandates, but Paisley saw a sense of community developing.

"A lot of people were upset, but for the first time ever . . . or the first time in two years, they had hope."

It was a level of patriotism you'd expect on Canada Day, not on a highway overpass in the middle of January. Paisley knew he wasn't done with the truckers. He went home, threw together a backpack, and the next day drove to Ottawa to join them.

Paisley's experience was similar to that of Dagny Pawlak, a 31-year-old former Liberal campaign staffer who went out to greet some of the truckers the same day as Paisley. Pawlak had been active in groups protesting COVID restrictions and mandates over the previous two years. On Thursday morning, she and her boyfriend went out with a group of volunteers to deliver food and other supplies to convoy truckers at the Flying J truck stop just off the 401 in London, Ontario. When she got there, she saw others had the same idea. People were showing up in droves with blankets, clothes, toiletries, and tons of food. She planned to drop off the donations and return home, but when she saw the trucks and the supporters filling up the truck stop parking lot, she called an audible. With just the clothes on her back—not so much as an extra shirt, she told me—Pawlak abandoned her plan to return home. She went to Ottawa instead. Pawlak and Paisley would soon become instrumental figures in the Freedom Convoy. Neither would go back home for weeks.

CHAPTER 4

THE RESPONSE

The convoy was immediately popular with large swathes of Canadians, but the media and most politicians were less impressed. The media was slow on the uptake, even as the convoy's organization, fundraising, and grassroots support grew. Early coverage tended to be regional in scope, focusing on groups of truckers mobilizing in particular locations, but not capturing the convoy's national scope. CBC British Columbia ran a story about a small convoy "protesting hazardous road conditions on the province's highways—it travelled from Surrey to Vancouver, a distance of about thirty kilometres—while ignoring the much larger and longer convoy against vaccine mandates hitting the road on the same weekend.[24] Except for a *Western Standard* article on January 17 trumpeting the "massive convoy" planning to head to Ottawa, it was only when Tamara Lich's GoFundMe campaign neared seven figures that journalists started to pay attention.[25]

Organizers were clear in Facebook posts and live streams, TikTok videos, and tweets that the protest was about all vaccine mandates, but this was rarely reflected in mainstream coverage. The *National Post* framed the protest as just being about the vaccine requirement for cross-border truckers.[26] So did a Global News BC report, which quoted an expert who was perplexed the truckers were protesting because they were given time to get vaccinated before the mandate went into effect, as though the convoy was about notice rather than the fundamental injustice of vaccine mandates.[27] The mainstream media either didn't grasp the convoy or simply wasn't interested in fairly portraying it. The better coverage came from smaller, independent outlets in communities that were home to some of the convoy's organizers. An article from Discover Weyburn, a news outlet in Weyburn, Saskatchewan, a city of 10,870 just a few hours from Chris Barber's hometown of Swift Current, did a better job summarizing the convoy's agenda than any of Canada's three national television networks. It included the organizers' distinction between a protest of vaccines and of vaccine mandates. "Let me stress too we aren't anti-vaccine, we're anti-mandate, I think a lot of Canadians are frustrated with the mandates, the government is telling us what to do when to do it and I think we're tired of that," the article quoted Barber as saying.[28]

The main ammunition for the convoy's critics came from a Canadian Trucking Alliance (CTA) condemnation of the movement. The trucking industry association, which represents thousands of carriers and owner-operators, initially opposed the cross-border mandate but was quick to distance itself from the convoy. In a January 19 statement, the CTA said it "strongly disapproves of any protests on public roadways, highways and bridges," encouraging anyone opposed to the mandates to take out their frustrations by signing online petitions or writing letters to members of parliament.[29] Days later, the CTA more forcefully slammed the convoy, claiming the "vast majority of the Canadian trucking industry is vaccinated with the overall industry vaccination rate among truck drivers closely mirroring that of the general public."[30] CTA president Stephen Laskowski told truckers the mandate wasn't going away, and the only way to cross the border was to "get vaccinated." The CTA never supported its claim that Canadian truckers had a vaccination rate similar to that of the general population. In fact, their earlier numbers said both Canadian and American truckers were notably less vaccinated as groups. On social media, some convoy supporters called CTA and Laskowski "sell-outs" and circulated screenshots of Elections Canada records showing decades-old donations by the CTA to the Liberals, and more recent Liberal campaign contributions from Laskowski.[31] These criticisms only grew when Laskowski issued a joint statement with Transport Minister Omar Alghabra and Labour Minister Seamus O'Regan—the former being the one who implemented the trucker vaccine mandate—promoting vaccination and pledging to work together for the betterment of Canadians and the trucking industry.[32] The statement didn't mention the convoy, but the timing was not a coincidence.

The CTA's opposition to the convoy became a trump card for others seeking to delegitimize the movement. It was used to assert that the convoy didn't really represent truckers, even though truckers came up with the idea and were at the core of the protest. Some critics noted that Lich, one of the most prominent faces of the convoy, wasn't a trucker. Others attacked her over her affiliation with the Maverick Party. Formerly called Wexit, the upstart western independence party has numerous members who support western separation from Canada. (Lich told me she was never a western separatist, but wants Alberta to have a more autonomous and independent place within confederation, similar to Quebec.) The Maverick Party said many of its members were supportive of the convoy but it was not involved in organizing it and had no connection to the fundraising campaign.[33] A trucking news outlet accused Lich of "a history of association with radical groups," based on her board position with the Mavericks and her support of the Yellow Vest protests in 2019.[34] Gerald Butts, a former advisor to Prime Minister Justin Trudeau, shared the TruckNews. com article and baselessly suggested donations to the convoy would be used for nefarious purposes. "An Alberta separatist has collected almost a million bucks on a GoFundMe page to 'support' trucker protests," Butts tweeted.[35] "Where will the money go?"

When it became clear to anyone with a computer how big the convoy was going to be, the attacks started. Sowing doubt about the money, as Butts did, was one strategy. This was exacerbated when GoFundMe, as part of its standard due diligence for large fundraising campaigns, put a hold on releasing donations while it confirmed with Lich how the money was going to be distributed. Others latched onto unsavoury details about people involved in the convoy, such as James Bauder and Pat King, even though organizers had repeatedly distanced themselves from King. The Canadian Anti-Hate Network, a self-appointed watchdog on "hate groups and hate crimes," launched its crusade against the convoy in late January, calling it a "vehicle for the far right":

> They say it is about truckers, and have raised over $6 million dollars on GoFundMe. But if you look at its organizers and promoters, you'll find Islamophobia, antisemitism, racism, and incitements to violence.[36]

The group's write-up focused heavily on criticisms of King, and comments from another live streamer, Derek Harrison, calling for

"[Canada's] own January 6 event," referring to the Capitol Hill riot in Washington, D.C. in 2021. Harrison, who was never involved in the convoy as an organizer, said he wanted to "see some of those truckers plow right through that sixteen-foot wall" of fencing around Parliament Hill. The Canadian Anti-Hate Network, which receives significant government funding for its research and advocacy, was often the lone source in media coverage claiming "far-right" or "extremist" elements in the convoy's leadership. A Google News search of the organization's name turns up 799 convoy-related articles, many of which repeat its accusations of "hate" fuelling the convoy.

A January 25 Global News article latched onto the "January 6" narrative. The article was a smorgasbord of the most unpleasant missives plucked from the dregs of social media comment sections rather than a representative sample of anything.[37] A few days later, Global followed up with another article, "Some trucker convoy organizers have a history of white nationalism, racism." This one took aim at a 2019 speech by convoy spokesperson Benjamin Dichter criticizing "political Islamism," a radical ideology that seeks to build states and governments around Islamic law.[38] A *Toronto Star* piece published a day earlier, also citing the Canadian Anti-Hate Network, revolves around a TikTok video posted by one of the convoy's road captains which contained the logo of the Soldiers of Odin, a Finnish anti-migrant group with connections to a neo-Nazi organization.[39] There were several examples of people in the convoy's broader orbit making concerning comments or having questionable or even unsettling affiliations, but it was notable how the media treated the exceptions as the rule. This despite Lich's, Barber's, and Dichter's clear and continued condemnations of extremism and violence.

Organizers were unfazed by the pushback, which they had expected. They cautioned supporters to stay above the fray and focus on the positive momentum behind the convoy. Negative news articles weren't dissuading people from showing up to support the truckers from overpasses or sharing images from the convoy on social media (notably TikTok and Instagram). If anything, the negative coverage only motivated people to look into it for themselves. When they did, they generally found normal folks waving Canadian flags and talking about freedom, rather than the hate and racism the *Toronto Star* claimed the convoy was all about. The protesters' mistrust of most media outlets was not without foundation.

The first sign of political over-reaction to the convoy came from Nova Scotia, which in the days trucks were headed to Ottawa took the unprecedented step of imposing a ban on "people who stop or gather alongside Highway 104, the Nova Scotia-New Brunswick border, or at the Cobequid Pass toll area in support of the 2022 Freedom Convoy." The ministerial directive also threatened to fine anyone who helps "finance, organize, aid, or encourage blocking the highway."[40] Nova Scotia later expanded its ban to include all roadways. By the time of the directives, the convoy had already passed through Nova Scotia, so it was a moot point, but was indicative of government responses to come.

* * *

The convoy's highest profile critic was undoubtedly Prime Minister Justin Trudeau, whose first acknowledgement of it came in a January 26 press conference, two days before the first trucks parked in front of his office on Wellington St. in downtown Ottawa. Trudeau claimed close to 90 percent of truckers were vaccinated and infamously dismissed the rest of them:

> The small, fringe minority of people who are on their way to Ottawa who are holding unacceptable views that they're expressing, do not represent the views of Canadians who have been there for each other, who know that following the science and stepping up to protect each other is the best way to continue to ensure our freedoms, our rights, our values as a country.[41]

By that evening, #fringeminority was trending on Twitter, joining other convoy-related hashtags that had already dominated social media for days. Even though Trudeau wrote off anti-vaccine mandate protesters as racists and misogynists in a September interview, his "fringe minority" comment gained far more traction, akin to Hillary Clinton's malignment of Trump voters as a "basket of deplorables" in 2016. The convoy's supporters embraced the attack: they were generally more amused by it than angered. In part, this was because they could look around and see the movement was neither small nor fringe. As organizer Brigitte Belton told me, it was hard to take the "fringe" label seriously when the truckers were seeing thousands of people cheering them on from overpasses and the side of the road at every stage of the trek to Ottawa. Manitoba road captain Dale Enns found it hilarious: "(Trudeau) said that and then you drive down the road and see how many people are out to cheer us on and support us," Enns said. "He was the fringe minority, because I would say more of Canada was behind us than behind him." What's more, added Enns, there was nothing "unacceptable" about the message of freedom.

If he wasn't already, Trudeau's comments ensured he was the villain in the convoy's story. The more hopeful convoy supporters thought they would get a hearing in Ottawa from the prime minister or at least someone in his government. Others knew it wouldn't be easy, which was why they planned to stick around until the mandates were gone altogether.

Optimism that the Conservative Party of Canada would lend a sympathetic ear were also dashed. A few days before Trudeau maligned the convoy as an unacceptable fringe minority, Conservative leader Erin O'Toole failed to give a straight answer on whether he would meet with the truckers in Ottawa, or whether he supported their goal. In one response, O'Toole said Canada needed to "tackle the supply chain crisis" and "encourage vaccination." Asked by another reporter if he supported the convoy, he said "I support getting as many people vaccinated as possible, including truckers." Subsequent attempts from reporters to get a clear response were similarly unsuccessful. O'Toole was on the record opposing the vaccine mandate for cross-border truckers—he supported alternatives such as rapid testing—but his statements generally hinged on the threat to the supply chain rather than whether vaccine mandates were just or unjust. With the convoy fighting for an end to all mandates, O'Toole's half-hearted criticism of only the trucker mandate wasn't winning anyone over. On the seventh or eighth attempt at an answer, he said it was "not for the leader of the opposition . . . to attend a protest on the Hill or a convoy." (In fact, politicians attend rallies on Parliament Hill all the time). Soon after, O'Toole fumbled his way through a CTV interview, pledging to meet with "truckers and with the industry," but conveniently leaving out whether truckers in the convoy would be among those graced with an audience.

Except for a few backbench members of parliament, the federal Conservatives had been generally silent throughout the pandemic on issues of lockdowns, vaccine mandates, and vaccine passports, and their silence persisted into the 2021 federal election. During that campaign, O'Toole largely sidestepped questions about ending restrictions by claiming they were under provincial jurisdiction and therefore not his problem. When Trudeau proposed federal mandates for air and rail travel and employment in the civil service, O'Toole opposed them, but focused more on accusing Trudeau of politicizing vaccination. Nevertheless, the feeling among unvaccinated Canadians, including truckers, was that the official opposition party did not represent them.

Yet the trucker vaccine mandate would be a turning point for the Conservative party. It gave them a wedge they could use against the Liberals. Ironically, Trudeau had legitimized his critics earlier in the pandemic by constantly exalting the importance of essential workers—especially truckers. In March 2020, for instance, he posted a glowing tweet about the "truck drivers who are working day and night to make sure our shelves are stocked."[42] He asked Canadians to "#ThankATrucker for everything they're doing and help them however you can." By the time the convoy was on the road, they had popular support among a broad cross-section of Canadians, and support from the Conservative party's base was virtually unanimous. O'Toole's refusal to support to the convoy frustrated several Conservative members of parliament.

Less than an hour after the January 24 press conference at which O'Toole failed to give a straight answer about the convoy, Alberta Conservative MP Martin Shields tweeted a video of himself standing by the Centennial Flame on Parliament Hill sharing how "eagerly" he awaited the opportunity to greet the truckers in Ottawa. Saskatoon Conservative MP Kevin Waugh went out to meet some truckers who were just about to join the convoy, posing for a photo beside one of them with "End the Mandates" decaled on the window. Alberta Conservative MP Shannon Stubbs, who had been relegated to the back of the backbench by O'Toole, implored her Twitter followers to "do whatever we can to show our support for the Convoy," while former Conservative leader Andrew Scheer thanked truckers in a tweet decrying Trudeau's attacks on "personal liberty." By the next day, O'Toole seemed like the only one in the Conservative caucus who wasn't on board with the truckers. The clincher was when his own deputy leader, Manitoba MP Candice Bergen, issued a statement of support for the convoy.

O'Toole was already on thin ice with a lot of his party's base for his poor showing in the 2021 vote, which many attributed to his failure to distinguish his policies from those of the governing Liberals. His unwillingness to support the convoy shattered what little ice remained.

On January 26, O'Toole published an op-ed in the *Toronto Sun* which a source in his office said was intended to signal support for the convoy. This may be true, but it curiously failed to include the word 'convoy,' and had a pitying tone. "Like you, these truckers have been through a lot over past two years (sic)," he wrote.[43] "So you can understand why they are protesting. I know you can. Canadians are empathetic and caring. It's in our nature, especially when we are witnessing first-hand the grief and uncertainty of so many people. Canadians have a right to be heard, not just in an election, but at all times, especially in these extraordinary circumstances." O'Toole then spent several paragraphs taking aim at unspecified "groups that would take advantage of the plight of truckers just to sow division and advance their misguided agenda," before imploring truckers to protest peacefully.

A day after the op-ed came out, O'Toole finally caught up to his party and released a video condemning the trucker vaccine mandate and supporting the right to peaceful protest while accusing Trudeau and the Liberals of trying "demonize" truckers. A day later, he posted a photo of himself meeting with truckers he said were on the way to Ottawa. The gestures were too little, too late for those involved in the convoy. Dichter, a former Conservative candidate, was annoyed the Tories wouldn't take the easy opportunity for a political win. "We were perfectly teed up for the Conservative party and they didn't take a swing," he said. "They keep doing that. Over and over again, chasing the Liberals off the cliff. And this was the most stark example of it."

O'Toole's embrace of the convoy was also too late for people in his party. Behind the scenes, members of the Conservative caucus were sharpening their knives. O'Toole would become the convoy movement's only political casualty.

PART II
THE BLOCK PARTY

CHAPTER 5

WELCOME TO OTTAWA

As soon as I arrived in downtown Ottawa, I could tell it was not the city I knew. I lived in Ottawa through the summer of 2009 while doing an internship on Parliament Hill. My great frustration with the city was its sleepiness. This Ottawa was loud. There were people and trucks all over the Hill and horns blared continuously. Not regularly—continuously. From the time I checked into my hotel room until I finally got to sleep, there was less than a minute of horn-free solace. The truck engines sounded silent by comparison. Even as someone enjoying the spectacle of it all, the novelty of the horns wore off rather quickly (for organizers as well, I later learned). Something big was happening, and I needed to be there to see exactly what that was.

I arrived on Friday, January 28, the day before the convoy was officially due. My (foolish) original plan was to drive into Ottawa to cover the convoy's arrival. I thought better of it a couple of days beforehand and flew up instead. I wasn't confident I'd be able to get my car into the city and was even less confident I'd be able to get it out at the end of the weekend. My taxi driver was initially wary of driving me to my hotel, citing the Ottawa Police Service's warning about unnecessary travel downtown. (He was listening to

CBC Radio, which might have contributed to his fear of going near the truckers). He eventually relented, with the caveat that he might not be able to make it to the Sheraton, where I was staying for the weekend. I picked it for its proximity to Parliament Hill, knowing the cold weather would have me going back and forth to warm up. Fortunately, traffic was still flowing on Albert St. so I didn't need to hike several blocks with my bags as the driver suggested I might.

Much like the streets, my hotel was buzzing on arrival. The front desk agent told me all the rooms were booked for the weekend—something the property hadn't experienced since before the pandemic. It was clear from the length of time it took my DoorDash dinner order to arrive later that evening that the streets were quickly filling up. The first thing I noticed was that Ottawa's mask mandate had seemingly evaporated. I didn't see a single masked hotel guest. One of the front desk clerks dutifully tried to hand out masks to new arrivals and those congregating in the lobby, but soon gave up. The truckers were taking over.

* * *

The convoy was supposed to roll into Ottawa on Saturday, nearly a week after the first bunch departed from Delta, B.C. Other groups from eastern Canada, Quebec, and southwestern Ontario were set to converge on the same day. Originally, the various convoys planned to meet outside the city and drive in together, but their itineraries had grown less reliable as the week progressed thanks to weather, traffic delays, and the sheer volume of trucks. It had amassed such grassroots momentum that truck drivers and other protesters were showing up in Ottawa on their own, eager to stake out prime real estate on Wellington St.—as close to Parliament Hill as possible. One organizer admitted to me that the weekend was a "logistics nightmare." In a perverse way, this wasn't such a bad thing. Many of the truckers wanted to disrupt the city, so the traffic jams only made the convoy more noticeable. Because of the delays in the official itineraries, the truckers who had the most prominent positions on Parliament Hill tended to be lone wolves.

While organizers had been abundantly clear that they didn't plan to leave Ottawa until Canada was free of vaccine mandates and vaccine passports, police and Ottawa municipal officials either weren't paying attention or thought they were bluffing. On Wednesday, Mayor Jim Watson said the city didn't know how many people were coming or how long they'd stay.[44] Things weren't much clearer by Friday, with Ottawa police chief Peter Sloly advising that demonstrations "will continue through the weekend and may continue into the following week."[45] An internal memo from the National Capital Region Command Centre, an intelligence-sharing effort between federal, provincial and municipal governments, predicted the convoy would leave "no later than" Wednesday, February 2.[46] An Ottawa memo blamed protest organizers for misleading police about their plans, although all the convoy leaders I spoke to told me they were as candid with police as they were with their social media audiences: they would be there as long as it took. Police nevertheless cooperated with the convoy, in some cases going above and beyond what organizers expected.

In fact, police officials who were in close contact with organizers in the lead-up to the convoy's arrival provided a nearby parking lot for the truckers' use as an overflow site. This was at Raymond Chabot Grant Thornton (RCGT) Park, a baseball stadium in

Ottawa's east end, about six kilometres from the Hill. On January 26, a police liaison officer texted one of the convoy organizers to tell him police had "secured" the lot for the convoy's use; it would be known as Coventry, after the road on which it is located. There was no discussion of length of stay at all. (That said, the owner of the baseball team that uses the stadium said police asked him if they could offer it to the convoy for one weekend).[47] The truckers turned the parking lot into a permanent encampment, which served as the convoy's staging area and fuelling depot. Organizers made sure to send a couple of reefers—trucks with refrigerated trailers—to the site to store food, although between donations and food bought ahead of time, they soon had more than would fit in the trailers.

On the Friday of the first weekend, everyone was treating parking rules around Parliament Hill as mere suggestions. Real parking spaces had been filled by Friday morning as protesters trickled and then flooded into the city, requiring creative solutions for those wishing to stick around. Convoy trucks initially reduced Wellington St. to one lane each way, but by 2:30 p.m. they had filled all lanes but one (for emergency access) for five blocks ranging from Lyon St. to Elgin St. Within an hour, north-south streets like Bank and Metcalfe also closed. Police restricted access to some streets, but it was the truckers who shut down most of them. It wasn't long before Ottawa's core looked like a truck stop and the protest was nowhere near over.

The Ottawa Police Service recommended that locals steer clear of downtown to avoid the traffic, more than any other reason.[48] Police were visible on the streets, although not in the numbers one might expect. They used a light touch on the protest, focusing more on keeping emergency routes open than anything else. (This was a goal shared by convoy organizers, many of whom had backgrounds in emergency response). A few officers even directed some of the trucks into place, including right on Wellington St. The Ottawa Police Service's primary concern was preventing a violent protest, not blocking the establishment of a semi-permanent truck stop. Its primary message to protesters was to keep things peaceful.

Most of the license plates I saw on Friday were from Ontario and Quebec, with a smattering of vehicles from further afield joining them.

* * *

By Saturday, trucks and cars filled not only the streets around Parliament Hill but most of downtown Ottawa. The protest sprawled in all directions, including down Rideau St. to the east and the John A. Macdonald Parkway to the west. Streets not filled by convoy trucks and cars were blocked by police barricades. Convoy vehicles that overnighted at a truck stop in Arnprior outside the city came in throughout the day, as did other convoy supporters in a steady stream. Vehicles that couldn't find places to park drove around, waving flags and honking horns. Other people parked away from the core and hitched rides into the main protest site—often from strangers. One of them told me a Canadian flag on a car was synonymous with the word "taxi."

As one would expect of Ottawa in January, the weather was not all that hospitable to outdoor gatherings—grey and gloomy with a temperature of -20 Celsius, but that wasn't stopping people from tailgating and welcoming new arrivals.

One of the first trucks to stake a claim on Wellington St. was André Landry's. Landry and his wife, Ann, arrived from Quebec at around noon on Friday, parking directly in front of the Peace Tower. He and his truck would remain in Ottawa for weeks. On Saturday, he was one of the more prolific honkers, eliciting cheers from the crowd every time he tooted his air horn. He told me he was there to support the people, pointing to the 18,000 assembled on Parliament Hill that weekend. As an unvaccinated trucker, they were there largely to support him.

People held up signs supporting freedom, opposing vaccine mandates, and making any number of unflattering comments about Justin Trudeau. Next to Canadian flags, black "Fuck Trudeau" flags seemed to be the most popular. "This is the first time in two years I've felt proud enough to fly this," one woman told me of her Canadian flag.

This was a common theme: several people told me the convoy restored their faith in Canada. Through the diesel exhaust, there was a hopefulness in the air that was far more discernible than the anger depicted in the media's convoy coverage. People didn't just protest for a return to normal but acted as though that normal had already returned. In many provinces at the time, unvaccinated people were barred from public spaces, including restaurants and gyms. For unvaccinated protesters, this was the first time in a while they were able to socialize freely without breaking a law or feeling like pariahs.

One volunteer told me it was the first opportunity in years for most people there to let their guard down. "(Thousands of) people in one spot, and they didn't know each other from a hole in the ground," he said. "But everyone respected each other. They loved each other. They shared everything they had. There was no judging anyone. No one even talked about Covid. No one talked about masks. They didn't care if you wore a mask. They didn't care if you were jabbed. It was just freedom of speech. There was no judgement. It was amazing. I've never been around so much love in my life."

It wasn't uncommon to see shinny hockey and snowball fights in the streets. In the evenings, people danced, often late into the night, with a DJ blasting music from the makeshift stage. At one point, a large circle of people held hands and walked around to the song "We Are the World," accompanied by an Indigenous drummer and off-beat truck horns.

For the most part, it was a space where no one cared about vaccination status, and people accepted each other as they came. An exception was the man going through the crowd offering a marijuana joint to anyone who deleted their vaccine passport from their phone in front of him. If they didn't have one to delete, he'd give them two joints. Several demonstrators openly identified, either on a sign or in conversation, as fully vaccinated, dispelling the widespread claim that it was an anti-vaccine protest. There were a handful of signs taking aim at COVID vaccines on conspiratorial grounds (Bill Gates, 5G, you name it), but these tended to be outliers. It was about mandates, not vaccines themselves. One sign that caught my eye read: *"FULLY VAXXED / BIPOC / PRO-CHOICE / ANTI-MANDATE."* It was held by a woman from Smith Falls, Ontario. She shook her head vigorously when I asked if she was politically conservative. She was no right-winger, and certainly no racist, misogynist, white supremacist. But she vehemently objected to how Trudeau had maligned those who, like her, simply opposed mandated vaccination.

The crowd's diversity was noteworthy. Quebec flags flew alongside Alberta flags; Indigenous flags flew alongside Canadian flags. Quebec at the time had proposed a tax on the unvaccinated, who were also prevented even from shopping at big box retail outlets. "J'veux aller au

Canadian Tire" ["I want to go to Canadian Tire"] one quintessentially Canadian sign proclaimed. Indigenous people, on average, are less likely to be vaccinated than non-Indigenous people, leaving them disproportionately affected by vaccine mandates. From some of my conversations with Indigenous protesters, they shared with other demonstrators a deep distrust of government control over individual decisions, particularly medical ones.

One of the more popular speakers on the opening weekend was Noeline Villebrun, a former Dene national chief and clan mother from Yellowknife, who made the journey to Ottawa and delivered an Indigenous blessing from the flatbed stage. "With our hearts that are up here on this stage, we thank you," she said, with Tamara Lich by her side. "Because that's what this movement is about. One heart. And what does that mean? That means love, understanding, acceptance, tolerance. And when we have that, we accept and we respect . . . one another."

A brief clip I shared of Villebrun's remarks on Twitter quickly amassed over 12,000 likes, and a long list of replies pointed out the curious juxtaposition of an Indigenous clan mother giving a blessing to a group that had been collectively identified as a bunch of extremists by the Prime Minister and some in the mainstream media.

* * *

While Chris Barber and the road captains had been responsible for getting the convoy to Ottawa, it was anyone's guess what the city would look like when they got there. Fortunately for the convoy, an arrival committee had been struck. It mobilized and rapidly expanded as the trucks neared. When Barber and Lich got to downtown Ottawa on Friday evening, they were shocked to see what was waiting for them. A team of Ottawa-based organizers had set up an operations centre at the Swiss Hotel, a boutique inn tucked away off the main streets, several blocks east of Parliament Hill. The convoy took over the hotel, operating day and night out of its basement. The Ottawa crew had originally intended to use the basement as a meeting place and rallying point, but it turned into a 24/7 command centre with computers, fridges, maps, and a volunteer caterer. The organizers even installed a dispatching program to facilitate communication and geographic tracking for 100 medics and security team members volunteering in the convoy. All of this was established within six days.

Taking the lead in pre-arrival Ottawa operations was Chris Garrah, who set up the Adopt-a-Trucker initiative. His core team in Ottawa included former RCMP officer Danny Bulford, an IT specialist, and a paramedic, as well as some 400 volunteers. While the convoy's initial GoFundMe campaign had raised millions to cover the fuel costs of participants, Garrah and his wife wanted to make sure other needs—like housing, clothing and food—were met. This was initially accomplished by the use of spreadsheets to pair individual truckers with individual donors. The approach was neither efficient nor scalable as people kept coming out of the woodwork with offers of spare rooms, meals, hotel credits, and so on. Garrah thus started the Adopt-a-Trucker fundraiser on the American Christian crowdfunding site GiveSendGo. It raised hundreds of thousands of dollars, money used to cover such set-up costs, like the computers for the Swiss Hotel, walkie talkies, medical equipment, portable toilets, some hotel rooms for out-of-town volunteers. And a couple of barbeques and 24,000 hot dogs.

"We were just basically making sure that they had showers and that we could provide them food, shelter, socks, underwear, toothpaste—whatever we could provide," Garrah said. "We had a team working night and day doing that."

The hot dog expenditure proved to be unnecessary. For the next three weeks, people would show up non-stop with food, in such volumes that protesters couldn't eat it fast enough. According to a couple of organizers, homeless shelters were turning away the excess food because it was too much even for them to distribute.

* * *

There wasn't a hard and fast programme set up for the convoy's first weekend in Ottawa. Some people not connected with the convoy organizers, like People's Party of Canada leader Maxime Bernier, arranged to give speeches and hold rallies around downtown Ottawa. But the protesters naturally wanted their own entertainment, which is where the main stage came in.

By a happy accident, a flatbed truck with a crane was prominently parked on Wellington St. at Metcalfe St., just a stone's throw from Trudeau's office and directly in front of Centre Block. This truck became the stage, with a Canadian flag hanging from the crane as a rallying point for the convoy. (At one point, a reporter mistook the weight hanging from the crane for a wrecking ball she suggested might threaten the building in which the Prime Minister's Office is situated).

Bethan Nodwell knew the stage would be a focal point, so she wanted to go all-out on sound equipment. Nodwell quit her job as a nurse in Wakefield, Quebec, in August 2021 over the healthcare system's handling of Covid. A few weeks later, her province announced a vaccine mandate for healthcare workers which would have jeopardized her job anyway (Quebec eventually backtracked on this when it faced a mass exodus of unvaccinated healthcare workers). Nodwell needed amplification that would project to thousands of people over truck horns, diesel engines, and wind. She also wanted a riser for media. Adopt-a-Trucker rented $40,000 worth of equipment at Nodwell's behest. (Soon they spent thousands more renting a jumbo video screen for behind the stage).

On the first Saturday morning, police would not let the sound gear through their perimeter. The organizers were told they did not have the correct permit, though they had been issued a protest permit for Parliament Hill. Bulford, the former RCMP officer, tried to negotiate, but to no avail. Nodwell learned that the New Blue Party, an upstart right-of-centre Ontario political party founded by Jim Karahalios, had some speakers set up at Major's Hill Park, a green space behind the Chateau Laurier hotel with a view of Parliament Hill. Nodwell led a group to the park and circulated word that the festivities would be moved there. The flow of foot traffic, however, was mostly in the opposite direction—towards Parliament Hill—which prompted the New Blue Party to move its sound system to the flatbed truck for the convoy's organizers to use.

The crane stage became a magnet for anyone and everyone who wanted to crash the party—and there were a lot of those. Organizers always stressed they wanted the convoy to be non-partisan and didn't want politicians co-opting the movement. That plea proved unenforceable within a matter of hours. Karahalios wanted to speak because his party had donated the sound system; Derek Sloan, the leader of the competing Ontario Party, wanted to speak because Karahalios did; Bernier wanted to speak because the PPC had previously been the lone federal party speaking out against vaccine mandates. On it went. Organizers welcomed other unplanned speakers. Rebel News founder Ezra Levant gave an impassioned, albeit off-the-cuff, speech about the importance of independent media; evangelical influencer Laura-Lynn Tyler Thompson got her moment before the throng; dissident doctors were also hot tickets. Nodwell, who expected she would be helping the convoy as a medic because of her nursing background, quickly became the stage manager for no other reason than she took charge when it was apparent someone needed to.

There were no stairs to get up on the stage—another indication of the by-the-seats-of-their-pants reality of the convoy's opening weekend. Volunteers scrambled to find crates to craft some makeshift steps. A more efficient method came from firefighters—of which there were dozens volunteering, many laid off because of vaccine mandates—who took turns lifting people on and off the stage. (One woman told me she lined up to speak only to get a boost from the "handsome fireman.")

Nodwell asked each prospective speaker the gist of his or her remarks before handing over the microphone. She wanted to weed out crackpots, but because it was a grassroots movement, she pretty much let anyone who wanted to speak do so. (This would later cause some friction between her and other organizers, particularly when she let Pat King take the stage.)

On Sunday morning, the stage was home to a worship service led by Henry Hildebrandt, a prominent anti-lockdown pastor from Aylmer, Ontario, and Carlos Norbal, a Quebec pastor who translated Hildebrandt's sermon and prayer to French. When the crowd was finished praying, they started chanting, "freedom!"

* * *

Shortly after the worship service, Benjamin Dichter, Lich, and Barber held a casual press conference in a guest room at the Swiss Hotel. Dichter curated the invitation list and allowed only a small group of independent and conservative journalists to attend, including Keean Bexte of the Counter Signal (whose video of the press conference a mainstream outlet later used without permission), a reporter from the National Telegraph, and columnist Rupa Subramanya of the *National Post*. I was among them. I didn't know at the time that it wasn't an open press conference, although Dichter told the assembled journalists that legacy media outlets were banned from attending for perpetuating fake news stories about the convoy. "We know if we had invited the *Toronto Star*, CBC—all these mainstream news organizations—they'll do what they always do . . . they'll come in with five people, and they'll have these giant cameras and they'll take up half the floor space and bully everybody else. That's not what this is about. This is about us coming together, talking to one another, answering any questions that you have." He said the organizers would give their media guests "all the time in the world."

Dichter admitted organizers had no idea how many truckers there were in Ottawa or en route. He put on the record that the trucks weren't going anywhere. "They're designed to be on the road . . . for an indefinite period of time," he said. "As long as you keep fuelling them, they can sit there for weeks and months. And now we have, what, $8 million? So $8 million worth of fuel. I don't know, 2023? 2024?"

CHAPTER 6

SETTLING IN

The convoy was a remarkably sophisticated operation despite its grassroots, blue-collar membership. Many of the convoy's leaders and key volunteers were current or former soldiers, police officers, doctors, nurses, and paramedics, many of them out of work because of vaccine mandates. The governments that fired these people for being unvaccinated had inadvertently created a large group with specialized skills, time to kill, and axes to grind.

"A lot of these people were trained in incident management, crisis management, special events management," convoy lawyer Keith Wilson said. "They replicated everything they had been trained to do, and it was remarkable, the way they came together. All these people who didn't know one another weeks earlier were working as this fine oiled machine."

Several of the organizers I interviewed spoke in battle analogies and tactical language to describe their operations. Tom Marazzo, a former Canadian Armed Forces captain nicknamed Army Tom by other organizers and leaders, had a sprawling map of downtown Ottawa on which he planned emergency routes and truck movements as though he were organizing an invasion of a warzone. For a time, the security team insisted people put their phones in a box outside their boardroom when meeting and swept the rooms for bugs. They never found any, but several organizers are convinced the Royal Canadian Mounted Police or Canadian Security Intelligence Service were spying on them. Tamara Lich switched hotels at one point when she saw a camera pointed into her room from an office building across the road. (She thought it could just as likely have been a journalist, but either way, she didn't want to deal with it).

Team leaders met at the Swiss Hotel, their main headquarters, each morning to update one another on developments from the previous day and action items for the day ahead. The room buzzed with activity. Security head Danny Bulford ran dispatch from the Swiss, as did the lead medic. There was an IT desk which managed the convoy's website and digital infrastructure; it periodically required defending against incoming cyberattacks. Social media and media relations were initially run out of the Swiss. There was an "intelligence" division as well, which was responsible for filtering and relaying information coming in from police and military sources, as well as political contacts. (One organizer claimed they received foreknowledge of some key political developments, as much as a week in advance). The finance team was headquartered in the Swiss, processing untold sums of cash donations using bill-counting machines, ledgers, and envelopes to distribute the money to truckers.

* * *

As the protest on the street grew, the organization behind the scenes had to evolve to deal with the mounting logistical, financial, and legal challenges. GoFundMe released $1 million to convoy organizers on January 28, satisfied with their plan to use the money specifically for fuel for truckers. The campaign cleared $10 million by February 2 and Tamara Lich, the convoy finance committee, and the crowdfunding platform continued working on a deal for the rest of the donations. GoFundMe transferred the first million into a personal account Lich held with TD Bank. She also received an additional $400,000 in Interac e-transfers directly from donors into another account. She managed to withdraw $26,000 for fuel and incidental expenditures.[49] However, soon after the million dollars from GoFundMe appeared, TD froze both accounts and then applied for a court order that would allow the bank to seize and refund the money in them.[50]

Convoy organizers registered a not-for-profit corporation on January 30, clunkily named Freedom 2022 Human Rights and Freedoms (they referred to it as "Freedom Corp"). Lich and Barber were named as directors, as well as Adopt-a-Trucker founder Chris Garrah, convoy spokesperson Benjamin Dichter, two road captains, and Chad Eros. Eros, an accountant from Moose Jaw, Saskatchewan, had just joined the team to manage the finances, a job that had grown enormously from when Lich had launched the GoFundMe campaign just two weeks prior.

By February 1, organizers were getting nervous about the lack of progress with GoFundMe and whispers that police might start laying charges against convoy protesters. They contacted the Justice Centre for Constitutional Freedoms, a liberty-minded legal charity, for assistance. The JCCF hired Keith Wilson to assemble and lead a legal team. Wilson thought about it for only a moment before agreeing, and packed a bag that night.

Wilson is an experienced litigator from Edmonton with a long resume and experience dealing with many of the areas of law he knew were likely to touch the convoy. He wasn't just a hired gun, but a true believer in the cause. He knew the legal situation was complex and multifaceted, but his top priority was working through the issues with GoFundMe and finalizing Freedom Corp's corporate status. He also thought the convoy needed a legal liaison with police, criminal lawyers on standby to respond quickly to potential charges, as well as litigators for other legal challenges that might arise.

Using money from Garrah's Adopt-a-Trucker campaign, someone chartered a plane to bring the lawyers and a couple others to Ottawa. The charter allowed the passengers, some of whom were unvaccinated, to sidestep the Trudeau government's vaccine mandate for commercial air travel. The morning of February 2, the plane left Calgary to pick up Wilson and JCCF lawyer Eva Chipiuk in Edmonton before detouring to Medicine Hat, Alberta, to fetch Lich's husband Dwayne. From there, it went to Saskatoon to pick up two more lawyers and to Regina for Eros. After stopping in Winnipeg for one more lawyer, the plane refuelled in Thunder Bay and advanced to Ottawa, where it landed at 11:30 p.m.

Upon arrival, Wilson set up his legal unit at the Arc hotel, where a second command centre was taking shape. Because the Arc was closer to the action on Parliament Hill, it was a magnet for protesters. People were coming and going all day. Some of them tried to insert themselves into the hierarchy and take charge.

As a result of its proximity to the protesters, the Arc command centre tended to deal with the immediate needs of the truckers, particularly those related to fuel. The Swiss would continue to manage big-picture files such as media relations, fundraising, security, and medical. Each command centre had its own culture and hierarchy, with the Arc's being the more chaotic of the two. Tamara Lich said that no matter when you went to the Arc, there always seemed to be a meeting taking place, and few people, including her, could figure out what, if anything, was being achieved by them. (The daily meetings at the Swiss were kept to twenty minutes before everyone dispersed and went about their business). Over time, the daily meetings at the Arc became occasions for truckers to air concerns and grievance with organizers. The meetings allowed for the sharing of information, particularly around fundraising which most truckers were otherwise reading about in the media along with everyone else. Communication between organizers and truckers was always challenging. The Arc meetings helped with this, and led to the implementation of a mass text message program to send updates directly to protesters (although word of mouth remained the most common communication channel).

In addition to the Swiss and Arc hotel hubs, the convoy sprouted a network of outposts around and outside of Ottawa. On Wellington St., one shipping container had been converted to a truckers' lounge, complete with block heaters, a snack counter, mini-bar, and a coffeemaker. The most significant site logistically was Coventry, the RCGT parking lot just east of Ottawa. Originally secured as an overflow lot for trucks that couldn't fit on Wellington St., Coventry became a fuel depot, campsite, food storage facility and receiving dock. Coventry also housed two large saunas a donor had dropped off with instructions to call him to pick them up when they were no longer needed. They were well used. Some people made Coventry their home and focused exclusively on what was happening there rather than downtown. Most protesters floated between the two, especially when it came to fuelling arrangements, which were critical for the convoy's survival given the consistently cold temperatures and the fact that most truckers spent their days and nights in their trucks.

For a grassroots movement, a lot of people within the convoy organization cared about titles. One key volunteer, an Ontario sheet metal worker named John (who didn't want his last name used), was assigned several of them, including head of procurement, head of fuel distribution, and head of logistics. He arranged to buy propane heaters, generators, and HotHands hand warmers, among other items. He was also responsible for the all-important fuel supply.

John learned about the convoy as it was on its way to Ottawa. On Saturday, January 29, he threw a sleeping bag, a couple of blankets, and a pillow in the back seat of his pickup and drove to Ottawa from his home in southern Ontario, planning to be there for one or two days. He had no plan and didn't know anyone. By chance, he ended up meeting convoy spokesperson Dagny Pawlak and her husband, who invited him to crash on the floor of their hotel room when they learned he'd be sleeping in his truck. They became fast friends, so when Pawlak couldn't make a meeting at the Arc, she asked John to go in her place. "Just say you're ground captain John with Adopt-a-Trucker," she told him. "These people just want a title. Trust me."

John didn't know anything about Adopt-a-Trucker, but he rolled with it. When people at the meeting questioned who he was, they seemed impressed by the title, even though it was a random string of words Pawlak had coined on the fly. Eventually, John was taking the lead on fuel distribution. He ordered two daily shipments of 3,500 litres of diesel from a sympathetic Ottawa vendor to Coventry. One arrived at 9:00 a.m. and the other at 1:00 p.m. From there, volunteers transferred the diesel to slip tanks on a fleet of up to a dozen pickup trucks specifically used for fuel runs. A coordinator arranged routes for the slip trucks to drive up to big rigs to fill their tanks, or when that wasn't possible to get as close as they could and transfer the fuel into jerrycans that volunteers would distribute on foot.

At first, John and his team set-up a fuel hotline for truckers to place orders, but with 300 calls and even more texts coming in daily, it proved unmanageable. Instead, fuellers took to canvassing the streets and fueling anyone with less than a quarter tank, a measure put in to ration fuel in the event of a police crackdown, which proved wise.

* * *

For the entirety of the convoy's time in Ottawa, there were dozens of trucks waiting outside the city to move in when they could. Sometimes a truck would come in to replace one that left Ottawa. Other times, word would travel about vulnerabilities in the police perimeter that could be exploited. These extra trucks had their own miniature encampments. One was in a crop field across from a truck stop in Arnprior, just outside of town. A couple were on private land off of exit 88 of the 417 highway (therefore nicknamed "88").

The Capital City Bikers Church in the Ottawa suburb of Vanier, closer to Coventry than to downtown, played a key role. The Pentecostal assembly was created to minister to bikers, but its "come as you are" approach to worship welcomed the convoy with open arms. The church, attended by a couple of the Ottawa-area organizers, housed the convoy's medical clinic. The convoy's lead medic, who did not wish to be named, put together a plan to address standard event-related medical needs. He proposed a team of mobile medics and four first aid tents—one at Coventry, one in Arnprior, one at 88, and one downtown. These would treat people for things like cold exposure, frostbite, and bad luck incidents like sprained ankles. When it became clear that the truckers weren't going home, the convoy's medical team opened a more permanent day clinic in the Bikers Church.

Protesters with serious needs were treated at the Bikers Church clinic by a rotating roster of 60 current and former nurses, paramedics and doctors (some licensed, others unlicensed). One man with a prosthetic leg received regular wound care at the church, according to two of his caregivers. The clinic also unconventionally treated convoy supporters who came down with COVID.

"We were running a bit of an illegal ivermectin operation underground," said Bethan Nodwell, a former nurse. "We were getting iver to people who needed it, who were starting to come down with COVID symptoms."

Ivermectin is an antiparasitic drug touted by dissident doctors as a COVID-19 treatment, although Health Canada says there is no evidence supporting its efficacy.[51] The use of ivermectin for COVID has been widely denounced by the medical establishment, which has only made it more sought after by those who oppose COVID vaccines. Early on, the clinic distributed veterinary grade ivermectin, provided by several farmers. Nodwell said some of the medical team members tried to find the human grade drug until out of the blue a volunteer "walked in with a bag full of it."

"So long as we were doing the appropriate weight, because it's assigned milligram-per-kilogram . . . we were able to distribute it amongst those in need," Nodwell said.

The medic was frustrated the ivermectin operation became as known as it did. Originally, the plan was to quietly supply the drug to convoy leaders who wanted it. Word travelled fast, however, and people were turning up at the Bikers Church and other first aid locations asking for it.

"It's like they don't understand the ramifications of inappropriate use or prescribing," the medic said, frustrated with how freely others shared the information (and his name) with me before I spoke to him. The medic was quick to note that most of the clinic's work was standard event-level first aid and not prescribing medicine or treating serious ailments.

* * *

The convoy had a head of procurement, but his job was made easy because things just kept showing up. This was true of the saunas at Coventry and the bouncy castles on Wellington St. which became the symbol of the convoy's block party vibe. Two Quebec men became known for their inflatable hot tub, which, given the consistently cold weather, was as functional as it was amusing.

One system that never got sorted out was the washroom situation. There were some portable toilets downtown and at Coventry, but not enough to accommodate the population surge on weekends as people showed up for a day or two to check things out. Moreover, organizers couldn't reliably get trucks in to empty the toilets, often facing police resistance. Fortunately, a combination of hotel rooms, private residences and sympathetic businesses provided bathrooms for the protesters to use. There were a few stalls constructed out of plywood behind a truck on Wellington, though. People had to read the rules before using them:

Fellas, #1 only. We have enough shit to deal with already. We don't need yours! #2—find a hotel.

Pee only. Poo elsewhere. And close the lid.

Bathroom issues notwithstanding, all the convoy's operations—from medical to administrative to culinary—came together quickly. One organizer remarked that it takes Ottawa a year to plan its big Canada Day party on Parliament Hill, and a bunch of "blue collar rednecks" did the same thing in under a week.

CHAPTER 7

WHO'S IN CHARGE HERE?

Convoy spokesperson Benjamin Dichter had an unenviable task. He had to inject message discipline into a disjointed group with a hostile media looking to exploit any weak links. He started each day at 6:30 a.m., scanning social media and convening colleagues to see what issues were trending. He arranged several press conferences similar to the one on the convoy's first weekend in Ottawa—with no mainstream media allowed—but spent much of his time trying to kibosh other press conferences various people and groups were holding, purporting themselves to represent the convoy. Some days, the messages of these competing conferences were as muddled as the cacophony of horns on Wellington St.

"Inevitably every day, about 8:00, 8:30, we would find out, oh, there's a press conference," said Dichter. "Great. We didn't authorize a press conference. Who authorized the press conference? So we spent an hour trying to figure out who authorized the press conference, where it's coming from."

Dichter broke his ankle a week into the Ottawa protest, confining him to a wheelchair with his leg in a cast. Stuck at his hotel, he wasn't always looped into discussions taking place at the Swiss and Arc hotels. He came to view press conferences that weren't scheduled by him as sabotage, either intentional or unintentional. The line between groups trying to help the movement rather than co-opt it wasn't always clear. Lich and others felt people were coming out of the woodwork to get a piece of the $10 million the convoy had raised.

A sore spot for numerous organizers was a February 3 press conference at the Marriott featuring Lich. It was announced a day earlier, assembled by a group called Taking Back Our Freedoms. There was one problem, however. Lich only learned about it when the press release announcing it went out. She had no connection to the group, which stationed itself in the Arc Hotel and inserted itself into the convoy's organizational team.

Unlike the official Freedom Convoy press strategy, which eschewed mainstream media, the Taking Back Our Freedoms press conference was open to anyone, including the reporters who had been publishing stories about the convoy's supposed association with white supremacy, racism, and so on. Lich didn't want to do it, but felt trapped because it had already been announced. She had only a few interviews under her belt, and no experience dealing with hostile media. To assuage her concerns, Taking Back Our Freedoms offered her some last-minute media training and arranged to have other people participating in the press conference to back her up. Even so, she felt it was minimal for what was expected of her at the press conference, which she thought was inadvertently setting her up to fail.

Taking Back Our Freedoms executive director Roy Beyer said he and his team, which included media consultants, had, in fact, discussed the press conference with the Freedom Corp board, including Lich. He said she never expressed any concerns about not being ready and that it wasn't until after the press conference he learned she felt like she had been, in her words, "thrown to the wolves."

Fortunately for Lich, Keith Wilson had just arrived. The Edmonton lawyer was a godsend so far as she was concerned. "I don't know what I would have done," she said. "I didn't even know what to expect."

When Wilson learned of the press conference, alarm bells went off in his mind. He took charge of the conference and introduced Lich to deliver a prepared statement, which was crafted by Lich with a lawyer and a doctor. Unfortunately, Wilson said, it *sounded* like it was written by a doctor and a lawyer, and required a hasty rewrite moments before the organizers had to leave for the press conference. Lich nervously read the statement, in which she pointed out how many countries around the world had removed all restrictions and reiterated the convoy's call for provincial and federal governments to end all mandates and restrictions.

"We will continue our protest until we see a clear plan for their elimination," she said. "Let me assure the people of Ottawa that we have no intent to stay one day longer than is necessary. Our departure will be based on the prime minister doing what is right—ending all mandates and restrictions on our freedoms."

After Lich's remarks, Quebec road captain Joanie Pelchat read a translated version in French and security lead Danny Bulford, the former RCMP officer, spoke about the peaceful nature of the protest and the open lines of communication between protesters and police. Wilson opened the floor to questions about the GoFundMe campaign. The first question, based on the premise that Ottawa residents were "terrified," was a demand to know when the convoy would leave Ottawa (even though Lich had just addressed that in her statement). After answering the second question, which was about the funding, Wilson ended the press conference and led the organizers out. Reporters hounded Lich all the way to the stairwell but Wilson had warned her and the others beforehand to keep walking no matter what.

The February 3 press conference provided a valuable lesson for the organizers, but controlling the message and streamlining communications remained a challenge. On February 9, I learned that Pastor Henry Hildebrandt, who'd been holding Sunday services on the flatbed stage, would be part of a "convoy press conference" alongside People's Party of Canada leader Maxime Bernier, Ontario member of provincial parliament Randy Hillier, and COVID-dissident doctors Paul Alexander and Roger Hodkinson at the Ottawa Marriott hotel. Both Hodkinson and Alexander are on the Taking Back Our Freedoms advisory board. Knowing Hildebrandt had been a convoy mainstay, I assumed this press conference was official, or at least as official as anything convoy-related could be. I sent an innocuous message to Dichter to confirm the location. It was the first he had heard of the press conference. Soon after, he sent out a release advising media of a press conference his group was hosting at the Sheraton at the same time, which forced the other group to postpone its event to later in the day.

Hillier was a particular thorn in the side of the organizers—many of whom shared unflattering comments about him. One said he was the "biggest source of all the problems." Several accused Hillier of trying to co-opt the convoy, and ultimately casting it in a bad light by straying from the focus of pushing for an end to vaccine mandates and vaccine passports through the democratic system. On the first weekend in Ottawa, Hillier removed one of the barricades on Parliament Hill that parliamentary precinct security had in place to control pedestrian traffic flow. At another point, he tweeted side-by-side photos of jerrycans of fuel beside missile heads with the caption "LET. FREEDOM. RING."

"What a dipshit," Dichter said of Hillier. "He's trying to get the protesters in trouble. Intentionally. There is Randy Hillier. That's what he really is."

Dichter's attempts at controlling the media availabilities had limited success, and the problem wasn't just from external groups, but also people inside the convoy's organization. Just a day before the Hillier event, Dichter felt blindsided by an impromptu press conference hosted by Tom Marazzo. Marazzo came to Ottawa to provide organization and logistical support for the convoy. He called himself a volunteer rather than an organizer, and according to Dichter, said he wanted to remain a ghost, working away behind the scenes. Fed up with people seeking the spotlight in Ottawa, Dichter was relieved. Until, that is, he saw Marazzo at a boardroom table flanked by Chris Barber, Brigitte Belton, Tamara Lich and several road captains, speaking on the convoy's behalf on a Facebook live stream. "I'm willing to sit at a table with the Conservatives and the NDP and the Bloc as a coalition," Marazzo said. "I'll sit with the governor general. You put me—put us—at the table with somebody that actually cares about Canada."

Marazzo's comments were widely interpreted in the media as seeking to oust Justin Trudeau and replace the government with some sort of junta involving convoy organizers and opposition parties. CTV said Marazzo was now the "face of the . . . Freedom Convoy."[52] Public Safety Minister Marco Mendicino accused the convoy of making "extreme statements . . . that would seek to incite the overthrow of the government through violence."[53]

Marazzo later told me he must "eat a bit of responsibility pie" for the statement, which he lamented did not come across as intended. He never sought to be a spokesperson, but said he was urged to make a public statement by some of the volunteers operating out of the secondary operations centre at the Arc. Morale was at a low point after a week-and-a-half of protest, with little progress at the federal government level. Instead of listening to the truckers, the feds had continued to vilify them. The strategy of only engaging with politicians in a position to immediately scrap mandates and passports was failing. Marazzo was exasperated and wanted to "get the ball rolling" by putting the convoy's concerns to anyone who would listen who might be in a position to do *something*.

"I didn't care what party came into the room and said, 'Look, I'm here on behalf of my party. What's your concern? I'm here to help. Maybe I can go back and convince the government or somebody else in Parliament to send some sort of a delegation,'" he said.

Marazzo never envisioned—or even thought possible—politicians forming a coalition with convoy organizers. His comment, however clumsily expressed, was a call for opposition parties to work together to hold the government accountable on the vaccine matters.

However well intentioned, it didn't go over well with Dichter and Dagny Pawlak, who were leading the media team. The next day, they sent out a press release stating only four people were authorized to speak for the convoy—the two of them, Barber, and Lich. The implication was that Marazzo didn't speak for the convoy, but this was a hard sell given both Barber and Belton had appeared with him.

Pawlak's name on that short list caught a lot of people by surprise. Even though she had been working with the convoy since the first weekend, she hadn't been a public spokesperson. When people

Googled her and saw her connections to the Liberal party, including a photo of her with Mendicino (the minister tasked with shutting down the convoy), conspiracy theories started swirling. She had previously worked as a field organizer for the Liberals, but became disenchanted with them after the 2015 election and moved on. This was no Liberal party infiltration of the convoy, just an evolution in views. Pawlak was surprised by the online backlash. She had spent the last two years active in anti-lockdown events near her hometown, and no one in Ottawa had made an issue of her Liberal past. Fellow organizers affectionately called her "Deep State Dagny."

Tamara Lich was more widely accepted as a spokesperson, but Belton, whose early persistence with Barber made the convoy a thing, resented how much of the limelight Lich occupied. Belton doesn't think Lich is a bad person, but insists the convoy was always supposed to be about the community rather than an individual, and that the fame got to Lich's head.

* * *

To Canadians watching from afar, the convoy was personified by the people and groups jockeying for microphones in hotel ballrooms. On the streets, it was a different story.

David Paisley was so inspired by the convoy when he saw it driving on the 401 through southwestern Ontario that he packed a go-bag and was in Ottawa the next day. When he arrived the first Friday, he didn't know anyone. He planned to head home Sunday, but, like so many others, the convoy consumed him and he was there until the end. While he never met Barber, Dichter or Lich, he played a pivotal role for the truckers. He was a block captain for Wellington St., meaning his days were spent networking and communicating with the truckers parked on the convoy's most visible stretch of road. He attended the daily meetings at the Arc with other block captains to pass concerns up the chain and get briefings he'd share with the truckers on his block. He also created Live From The Shed, an online channel broadcast from a wooden shed on the back of a truck. His channel streamed live video from Wellington St. and interviews with people in the convoy protest.

I've liberally used the word "organizer" to describe those with key roles in the convoy, but the word is used loosely, and was at times a controversial label within the ranks. Attacks on the convoy from politicians and the media often involved elevating people who didn't deserve the designation to the role of "organizer" in order to cast the movement in a negative light. Some of the bona fide organizers, either out of humility or because they didn't want negative attention from media and law enforcement, distanced themselves from the label, even when they had a track record of actions you would be hard pressed to call anything but organizing.

Paisley rolls his eyes when asked about the "organizer" label, having seen how malleable and loaded a term it is. He was never assigned a task. He just showed up and started working. Paisley channelled psychologist and author Jordan Peterson's "hierarchy of competence" model to explain the organic nature of the convoy's structure. "It wasn't a hierarchy of job titles or anything—it was of competence," Paisley told me. "You connect with one person, realize they're incompetent and bump them down your scale of who to communicate with. Then you'd reach someone else and they seem quite competent so you'd start connecting with them, and then competent people would connect with other competent people and eventually you'd have a network of competent people who got things done."

And that's what Paisley did. He understood the visual importance of Wellington St. and wanted to make sure the truckers there were looked after. He started canvassing the street to meet all the truckers parked on it. They invited him into their cabs where they'd speak, often for long periods. In these conversations, he heard common questions like "How are we going to get fuel?" Paisley would answer: "Whoa, I don't know what's going on either. I just showed up." But he wanted to help find the answers, in part because he "got bored waving a flag pretty quick."

Paisley made a point of getting names and contact information to keep in touch through group text messages, saving contacts in his phone based on first names and skillsets like "Sam Mechanic" or "Jim House We Can Use." He took it upon himself to be the "eyes and ears" for the truckers, building a network of drivers and volunteers. Eventually, a small group of them met in a wooden shed affixed to one of the trucks, swapping notes and trying to figure out what was going on—and what needed to be going on. This proved vital because of how many people wanted to help but weren't tied into the organized networks like Adopt-a-Trucker or the Swiss Hotel team. One man stayed in his hotel room at the Sheraton from 8:00 a.m. to 5:00 p.m. each day to let in truckers who needed to take a shower. An older couple used their car to ferry people back and forth between downtown and Coventry. Countless people—often elderly ladies— cooked and baked, while a key group offered mechanical services.

Mike Nodwell one day went to the Arc with his wife in search of a printer. They had letters from friends and neighbours back home in Alberta that they wanted to give to their member of parliament,

John Barlow. Someone pointed him to a printer in a box and told him he could set it up and use it, which he did. Afterwards, other stuff needed printing, so he lent a hand. Before long, he was a full-time volunteer in the Arc, making coffee, delivering food, liaising with hotel management, and sitting in on planning meetings. All because he needed to print something.

The common thread between most of these people is that no one asked them to do anything, let alone assigned them roles. They just started helping. Many of these folks were fans or supporters of Lich and Barber, but they weren't taking their marching orders from them or anyone else. Some even had less favourable views of them, with one trucker describing the convoy spokespeople and fundraisers as the "corporate suit types" taking the glory while the truckers did the heavy lifting on the streets.

Media often tried to paint the convoy as a top-down organization with a firm hierarchy. As a result, outsiders never quite grasped that the organizers doing the interviews and controlling the fundraising weren't pulling the strings on the people on the ground. They couldn't have if they'd wanted to. The movement's grassroots nature was unshakeable.

CHAPTER 8

DUELLING NARRATIVES

On my way to Ottawa, I'd heard little in the media about the convoy beyond predictions of a violent insurrection and accusations of racism and extremism. Walking around downtown Ottawa the first weekend, I was relieved, though not surprised, to see nothing of this nature. I spent my time talking to people and taking in the sights on the streets and taking breaks from the frigid weather in my hotel room every couple of hours where I'd also recharge my rapidly draining cell phone. On one of these breaks, I looked at Twitter and was baffled to see what was trending in the online convoy discussion. A Terry Fox statue across the street from the Prime Minister's Office had been desecrated. A drunken woman had danced on the Tomb of the Unknown Soldier. Truckers had stolen food from a homeless shelter. And a man flying a Confederate flag had made his way through the crowd, as had another man with a swastika flag. These stories were all the rage online, but felt a world away from the block party atmosphere on the ground.

At the convoy press conference the first Sunday, Benjamin Dichter laughed it all off as "fake news." The "defacing" of the Terry Fox statue, reported by multiple media reports, was harmless: protesters had put a baseball cap on Fox's head and tied a Canadian flag around his neck as a cape.[54] They also placed in his arms a sign reading "MANDATE FREEDOM." All of these were easily removed with no damage to the statue. Nevertheless, the incident lived on in the comments of politicians and journalists as an example of convoy lawlessness.

Sometimes, it would take months to learn the truth behind a story impugning the convoy. There was indeed a video of a woman dancing on the Tomb of the Unknown Soldier. It received widespread criticism across the country. It wasn't until more than two months later that Ottawa police admitted the woman had no association with the convoy.[55]

On February 6, an Ottawa man named Matias Muñoz published a Twitter thread accusing two arsonists of bringing a "full package of fire-starter bricks" into the lobby of his downtown Ottawa apartment building at 5:00 a.m.[56] One of the would-be arsonists admitted to being part of the convoy, Muñoz wrote. The tweet received more than 12,000 retweets and the incident was raised in the House of Commons by NDP leader Jagmeet Singh, Liberal MP Mark Gerretsen, and other MPs as an example of "violence" within the convoy. It wasn't until March 21, more than a month after the protest had been disbanded, that police confirmed there was no connection between the suspects and the trucker protest.[57] After the statement from Ottawa police, Muñoz blamed the convoy for creating "a lawless scenario in Ottawa's core that acted as a catalyst for this arson attempt to occur."[58]

One of the most damaging stories was the allegation that truckers had harassed people at the Shepherds of Good Hope, a downtown Ottawa shelter and soup kitchen. The charity said in a January 30 statement that trucks had parked in its ambulance drop-off zone, and that protesters subjected soup kitchen staff and volunteers to "verbal harassment and pressure" to give them food.[59] The statement said the soup kitchen was "not certain of exact numbers," but that the incidents spanned several hours. While many of the organizers I spoke to were skeptical of the story, it was not altogether implausible. Food was difficult to come by that first weekend if you didn't know where to look. Many downtown restaurants, including those in the Rideau Centre, a nearby shopping mall, pre-emptively closed. (The ones that stayed open made small fortunes, however). The food tents under which volunteer cooks fried chicken wings, grilled hot dogs, and roasted whole pigs had been set up quickly but did not yet have the capacity to feed the tens of thousands who turned up on the first weekend. In any event, the incident was a one-off, and not representative of general protester behavior. Convoy organizers prided themselves on feeding the homeless over the next three weeks.

And then there were the flags. One masked man walked through the crowd on Parliament Hill holding a Confederate battle flag with a transport truck on it. A still image of the man circulated quickly, particularly among journalists, who devoted entire stories to it. A less-viral video of the man walking around shows other demonstrators heckling him and chasing him out of the crowd.[60]

The swastikas were even more curious. One photo shows a man in the distance—not amid the protesters on Parliament Hill or Wellington St.—with a swastika flag on a pole. My colleague Candice Malcolm of the pro-trucker media outlet True North put out a $6,500 bounty for information that could identify the flag-bearer. She wanted to ask what he was thinking.[61] Nothing substantive ever came of it. Was he an anti-convoy agitator or a genuine Nazi sympathizer? Both are possible. A handful of other swastikas appeared amid the protests, although typically in the context of demonstrators ham-fistedly accusing the Canadian government of being Nazis. This does not excuse the reprehensible use of such a hateful symbol at a protest, but there is a difference between Nazi sympathizers and people who are too dumb to come up with a more sophisticated argument than calling political opponents Nazis. That nuance was missing from the coverage.

I ran into Conservative members of parliament Michael Cooper and Damien Kurek, both from Alberta, handing out coffee to convoy protesters and conducted an impromptu interview with them. As we were setting up the shot, Cooper kept looking behind himself. I later learned it was because he had earlier spoken to the CBC while someone in the background carried a Canadian flag with a swastika sketched on it. A screenshot of that image had gone viral, which was when Cooper learned of it. CBC later ran a story on how Cooper was "under fire" for being in the vicinity of whoever the flag-waver was.[62]

On slower days, convoy critics got creative. CBC did a radio segment about why "freedom" isn't necessarily a nice word because it "thrived among far-right groups."[63]

The reality was that the main media narrative was already set, and the convoy's critics didn't care much about truth if a rumour felt like it fit. Canadian Anti-Hate Network chair Bernie Farber tweeted out a photo of a wildly antisemitic flyer "taken by a friend in Ottawa at the Occupation."[64] He labelled the convoy "the worst display of Nazi propaganda in this country." [65] As Quillette editor Jonathan Kay pointed out, the photo appeared on Twitter weeks earlier when it was snapped by someone in Miami with no connection to the convoy. Farber is not a random Twitter troll. He's testified in Parliament and is a regular on the CBC. Journalists and politicians ran with his story unquestioningly. NDP member of parliament Charlie Angus said the convoy's supposed extremism "isn't hidden, it's right there in the open." Justin Trudeau went so far as to accuse Jewish Conservative MP Melissa Lantsman of standing with "people who wave swastikas."[66] Liberal member of parliament Ya'ara Saks said that "honk honk," the convoy's online rallying cry, was actually code for "Heil Hitler."[67]

Even if the unfortunate incidents were all accurately represented, which they weren't, they were still marginal events in a massive protest involving tens of thousands of people whose time in Ottawa was marked by peaceful demonstration and celebration. Convoy spokesperson Dagny Pawlak wasn't surprised that the media elevated the one-offs to the status of major stories. "The mainstream media will find that one potentially toxic element and portray that as representative of the entire movement," she said. "That's something we didn't want to give them." But organizers couldn't control every person in a crowd that size.

The racist, extremist narrative embraced by many in government and the media subsumed a lot of interesting individual stories from among the protesters. Some of the most tremendous reporting in the convoy came from Rupa Subramanya, an economist and *National Post* columnist who spent almost every day walking around the Wellington St. camps talking to people about who they were and why they were there. "I have spoken to close to 100 protesters, truckers and other folks, and not one of them sounded like an insurrectionist, white supremacist, racist or misogynist," Subramanya, a woman of colour from India, wrote in an essay on the popular Bari Weiss Substack.[68]

It was strange that such a simple tactic—talking to the people involved in the protest—seemed radical in this landscape of media coverage. Subramanya identified that the protest, while ostensibly focused on vaccine mandates and passports, had morphed into an outlet for broader frustrations with government intrusion into personal lives. It was telling, to her, that many of the protesters she interviewed were immigrants from communist dictatorships who felt Canada was no longer offering the freedom they had fled their home countries to find.

In the city-within-a-city that the convoy created, people found the freedom and normalcy they craved, which speaks to why so many of them stuck around after intending to spend just a couple of days in Ottawa. Some found far more than that: trucker Tyler Armstrong, whose baby blue Kenworth was parked on Wellington right in front of the Hill, met and fell in love with protester Ashley Wapshaw at the convoy. Volunteers Bethan and Mike Nodwell, who didn't know each other before the convoy, met and learned they were cousins. One man I spoke to told me he found faith through at a ministry in Ottawa. Critics might write these off as isolated incidents, but they were more representative of the convoy experience than the isolated negative ones presented by the media and picked up by politicians.

Some of the most popular coverage I did in Ottawa came from simply streaming live video as I walked around. A few of my supporters told me they were so distrustful of the media's depiction of the convoy that they enjoyed the simplicity and honesty of a live feed of what was happening on the ground, even if what was happening was, at a particular moment, nothing important.

In fairness to the media, some reporters did their best to go out into the (often hostile) crowd to talk to people. Two standout examples were Evan Solomon of CTV and Sean O'Shea of Global News. Both of them had real conversations with people and stood there and took it when folks screamed at them. As a journalist with a conservative media outlet, I was largely spared the nastiness directed at a lot of mainstream media folks, which was difficult to watch and, as I told a couple of protesters, only furthered the negative depictions of the convoy in the press. I understood where the anger was coming from, having seen the media's vilification and misrepresentation of the convoy, but this didn't excuse the appalling behaviour of individuals attacking journalists who were trying to do their jobs.

* * *

Dichter was convinced that by misrepresenting the convoy, the media was exposing itself as biased. Especially the Canadian media. Foreign media, including conservative outlets like Fox News in the United States and GB News in the United Kingdom, were more open to the convoy in their coverage, as were foreign mainstream outlets such as the *New York Times* and the BBC. But the problem for the convoy's communications team remained: if facts on the ground weren't being reported fairly, there was no way the convoy's overarching message would be heard in Canada.

On February 15, Dichter appeared on Jordan Peterson's podcast to deliver a statement on the convoy's goals and values:

> The freedom convoy is a peaceful and loving demonstration based on the principles of unity and respect for all Canadians. We have come to Ottawa with two very simple demands: one, the government end all COVID mandates; and, two, the federal government remove its digital COVID tracking app called ArriveCan as a requirement to re-enter Canada.

We have not anticipated the thirst for freedom in all Canadians after two long years of restrictions and harsh lockdowns, which, in the minds of sensible Canadians are not in the spirit of the Charter of Rights and Freedoms and our esteemed constitution. The supporters of our convoy have come from all walks of life, and have been a source of unification for Canadians from across all provinces and cultures. We are not a group interested in identity politics or racial divisions. We are, in fact, open to all people who want to share their love, and help with the revival of the Canadian identity.

The freedom convoy leadership spans the country and comes from various Indigenous, rural and urban communities, all who have an ambition for unification and freedom. Our demands have not changed from day one: end the mandates and end the passports, and we will all go back home to our communities and our businesses and help Canada heal from the COVID years.

There have been many demands attributed to us that are not our demands, primarily from the legacy media. We do not want to overthrow the government. We do not want to remove any of our elected officials from power—that's what elections are for. We do not want to confront. We do not want confrontation with the good people of law enforcement, within our organization and within our crowds, we have countless first responders and military veterans who are all proud of the Ottawa police. We do not wish for military action. We want nothing other than for our peaceful and loving demonstrations, as well as our community outreach, to help inspire our fellow Canadians to have a voice and to appreciate the freedoms which we are fortunate enough to have and which many others in the world struggle to achieve.

We also would ask that our political class and the legacy media tone down their rhetoric. The era of slander and indiscriminately labeling fellow citizens with pejoratives or as racist needs to come to an end. We need to talk openly and respect one another. But we cannot achieve this if our political class continues to behave in such an unparliamentary manner, while the legacy media attacks the very people they're supposed to reach.

The unifying goal that all Canadians have is we want to return to a normal life – a free life, no matter where one lies on the political spectrum. Now is the time, and the first courageous step would be for the federal government to remove these divisive policies of mandates, and data tracking of our citizens. Allow us all to heal together.

Peace, love and unity is the future of the Canadian identity. Let's inspire the world to follow us on this journey of enlightenment.[69]

There was nothing new in Dichter's statement, although it was probably the clearest statement of the convoy's intentions uttered by any source during the three weeks. That he needed to deliver it suggests the convoy's message, in fact, was not being heard. Looking back on it, Dichter attributed the messaging problems to the grassroots nature of the movement. "If everybody stayed on the same team and on message, that narrative would have been increasingly more difficult for the mainstream media to spin," he said.

Pawlak agreed that "people shooting off on the sides" was the major source of messaging problems, but she wished the convoy media representatives had engaged, rather than boycotted, the mainstream media to counteract this. Convoy supporters lit up when CTV reporter Glen McGregor, refused admittance to a convoy press conference, was asked by hotel management to leave the premises, but the incident did nothing to advance the convoy's message. "The way I saw it was that, hey, they're likely going to misrepresent this anyway, so why give them an incentive to go get their story from other sources," said Pawlak. She thinks there would have been more to be gained with a strategy of taking media calls, "answering the questions to the best of my ability, keep telling them exactly what I'm telling you and anybody else and then just see what happens."

Pawlak also regretted that so much time and effort were spent dealing with internal conflict in the first week, and not enough putting together a concrete, proactive media plan. Even without this, the convoy was getting results.

CHAPTER 9

THE CONVOY EFFECT

Regardless of what media was reporting, the truckers enjoyed momentum and a great deal of popular support throughout their protest. Especially on apps like TikTok and Instagram, they tapped into a unique demographic of people who weren't all that political but nevertheless supported the convoy. Their appeal extended not only across Canada, but around the world. A coterie of anti-establishment celebrities rallied to their side. CEO Elon Musk got hundreds of thousands of likes for a January 27 tweet stating that "Canadian truckers rule."[70] The comedians Rob Schneider and Russell Brand cheered them on. Donald Trump Jr. posted a four-minute Facebook video praising the "heroic" truckers standing up for "medical freedom."[71] And former president Donald Trump received a standing ovation at the Conservative Political Action Conference when he pledged to stand with the truckers and Canadians "in their noble quest to reclaim their freedom."[72]

Organizers realized how big the movement was becoming when they saw copycat convoys crop up elsewhere. In early February, a group of American truckers launched a Facebook group promoting the "Convoy to DC 2022." They collected more than 100,000 members before Facebook deleted the group, supposedly for its links to the conspiracy movement QAnon.[73] American truckers regrouped and launched the People's Convoy, a weeks-long protest that travelled to and encircled Washington, D.C.

The US was no outlier: convoys set out for Wellington, New Zealand; Canberra, Australia; Paris, France; London, United Kingdom; and Brussels, Belgium, among other world capitals. All of them were inspired by the Freedom Convoy in Canada. The phrase "Canada-style protest," possibly never uttered before, appeared in eighty news articles in February. Seeing other groups around the world emulate them was great for the morale of the Canadian truckers, but the people the convoy needed to convince to lift vaccine mandates were federal and provincial politicians.

Plenty of politicians talked about an end to the pandemic and an eventual return to normal without giving anything resembling a timeline. Policies were all over the map. Some provinces, notably Quebec, were adding restrictions while most others seemed to be lifting them. But on the Tuesday after the convoy first landed in Ottawa, Quebec dropped a bombshell: it was abandoning its contentious (and possibly unconstitutional) plan to tax the unvaccinated.[74] The "health contribution," as the province called it, had been announced less than a month earlier, with officials maintaining that unvaccinated Quebecers were more likely to wind up in hospital and run up healthcare costs, so they should have to pay. The vax tax was followed by another announcement barring the unvaccinated from big box retail stores. Convoy organizers credit these policies, as well as Quebec's Covid curfew, which let police fine anyone out after 8:00 p.m. (later changed to 10:00 p.m.), with the strong showing of Quebec truckers and protesters on Parliament Hill. Yet it took only a few days of honking horns in Ottawa for Quebec to backtrack.

Premier François Legault, who had earlier seemed proud of enacting some of the harshest Covid restrictions anywhere, said he was now trying to avoid division and polarization in society. Needless to say, the convoy took this as a big win, the first of several.

On February 8, Alberta's premier, Jason Kenney, announced an immediate end to his province's vaccine passport program, and set a date of March 1 to lift its mask mandate.[75] Later that same day, Saskatchewan's premier, Scott Moe, followed Kenney's lead, announcing a February 14 end to vaccine passports. "It's time to heal the divisions over vaccination in our families, in our communities, and in our province," he said.[76] A few days later, Ontario's premier, Doug Ford, said a plan was in the works to drop Ontario's vaccine passport.[77]

All of these premiers were quick to downplay what quickly become known as the Convoy Effect. These things were already happening anyway, they insisted, but it wasn't a wholly convincing argument. Before the convoy, politicians had refused to give timelines, let alone put concrete reopening measures in place. Convoy organizers were not wrong to see these as wins for the movement. "Every day there was like a little head that would get chopped off, but not the big one that we were going for," convoy volunteer Bethan Nodwell said.

The big one was an end to all mandates and passports at all levels of government, especially the federal level. Organizers hoped someone from the governing Liberals, even a cabinet minister or senior staffer, would agree to meet them, but this was increasingly unlikely the more the convoy dug in and the more Trudeau railed against the anti-vaccine mandate protesters.

That there was no real opposition in the House of Commons during the early part of the protest served the prime minister well. For nearly two years, federal politicians had stressed a "Team

Canada" approach to the pandemic. Unity seemed more important to the Conservative and New Democratic opposition parties than pushing back against government policies that, like any government initiatives, could have benefitted from rigorous challenge. Before the federal leaders' debate in the 2021 election, all five party leaders set aside their disagreements to record French and English public service announcements urging Canadians to get vaccinated. That most Canadians did get vaccinated confirmed in the minds of the politicians that rising above partisanship had been the right thing to do, but the unvaccinated saw their unity as proof that no one in federal politics was interested in representing them. People's Party of Canada leader Maxime Bernier was the lone voice against mandates, but despite his party tripling its vote share from 2019 to 2021, it elected no representatives to parliament.

As noted earlier, the consensus in Ottawa began to fray when several Conservative MPs spoke out against the cross-border vaccine mandate for truckers. By the time the convoy hit Ottawa, it was evident that rank-and-file conservatives were broadly sympathetic to the movement, and more Conservative MPs were showing support, including the deputy party leader Candice Bergen. When leader Erin O'Toole dithered, the pro-trucker element in his caucus made its move. On the evening of Monday, January 31, dozens of Conservative MPs signed a letter calling for a caucus vote on O'Toole's leadership. At a tense marathon session two days later, they voted 73-45 to oust him. Caucus concerns with O'Toole's leadership predated the convoy and even the 2021 election, but O'Toole's lacklustre response to the truckers made it easy for the MPs to pull the trigger. "The ground is starting to tremble," a post on the Freedom Convoy Facebook page said.[78] "Can you feel it yet?"

Conservative MPs elected the pro-convoy Candice Bergen as their interim leader, and the first politician to launch a campaign to replace O'Toole as permanent leader was Pierre Poilievre, a darling of the convoy who, days earlier, had scoffed at reporters who attempted to dismiss the protest based on actions and comments from a few bad actors.[79]

Needless to say, Bergen's Conservative party didn't view the truckers as a fringe group. On February 4, just two days after she was elected interim leader, Bergen issued a statement asking truckers to remain peaceful but assuring them "Canadians and Conservatives have heard you loud and clear."[80] The same day, Bergen tried to set up a meeting with Tamara Lich. It was brokered by Lich's member of parliament, Conservative Glen Motz of Medicine Hat—Cardston—Warner. Motz called Lich to ask if she could go to a nearby A&W for a five-minute meeting with Bergen. Because of the public location, Lich and her team felt it would be no more than a photo op. Lich handed the phone to convoy lawyer Keith Wilson to play bad cop. To test their theory, Wilson responded with a counteroffer—an invitation for Bergen to meet with Lich at the Arc for a private conversation with no photos and no media statement. Either Motz didn't deliver the message or Bergen's office declined, but the meeting never took place. (Neither Bergen nor Motz responded to requests for comment.)

The convoy organizers' decision to not take the meeting is perplexing: they took ownership of the political shakeup that thrust Bergen to power, and photos of an audience with the leader of Her Majesty's Loyal Opposition would send a strong message to naysayers that the convoy had secured a seat at the table and was a mainstream political movement, rather than Justin Trudeau's "fringe minority." Evidently, the organizers didn't see it that way. Wilson understood they were giving up a potential boost in legitimacy, but felt the risk of a photo op turning the movement into a partisan one was a greater concern. "To the extent it has even been an organization, it has been trying to be apolitical," Wilson said.

Benjamin Dichter called the Conservatives "completely incompetent" for not accepting the Arc meeting, during which, he claimed, he and his fellow organizers would have helped the party "leverage the convoy" for political gain.

In any event, Bergen's office and the higher levels of the Conservative party never engaged with convoy organizers again.

* * *

For all the work that convoy organizers were putting into managing logistics, messaging, and other details, they remained at the mercy of the convoy's organic, grassroots momentum. What made it such a powerful political force also brought high degrees of political risk. To understand how the convoy could take on a life of its own, one need look no further than the border blockades. The same weekend the main convoys arrived in Ottawa, a group of truckers blocked the Canada-United States border crossing near Coutts, Alberta. The crossing is responsible for $15.9 billion each year in cross-border trade—or $44 million a day.[81] A few dozen truckers brought it to a standstill.

Coutts was just the beginning: other blockades developed in Surrey, British Columbia; Emerson, Manitoba; and the critical Ontario-Michigan bridge crossings at Sarnia and Windsor, among other locations. This was similar to the original idea of simultaneous national protests, jam-ups, and slow-rolls envisioned in December by early convoy organizer Brigitte Belton. But neither she nor the convoy protesters had anything to do with the border blockades. They just happened.

"We'd find out about the border closures from the media," Wilson said. "If these truckers thought it was a good idea to block a border, they would have driven to the border. They wouldn't have driven across the country in winter to go to Ottawa."

It was "purely a spontaneous, sympathetic movement," added Wilson. In all the meetings he had with organizers at the Arc and Swiss operations centres, he never heard anyone so much as talk to someone involved in a border blockage, let alone choreograph one. But that doesn't mean they weren't supportive of it, at least at first.

"I wish we could take the credit for the blockades, but we cannot," Lich said in a February 14 Facebook video.[82] "This movement has captured the hearts of Canadians and the entire world. We're aware that Canadians nationwide are feeling inspired by the truckers' resolve here in Ottawa and are starting their own convoy demonstrations as a means of showing support for ending mandates. We wish them well and are so heartened to see how organically this movement is spreading. We, of course, encourage all demonstrators across the country to be peaceful, just like we have been and will continue to be here in Ottawa."

She didn't write the statement she read in the video. She later said she was uncomfortable with some aspects of the border blockades, which she viewed as fundamentally different from the situation in Ottawa. "We were trying to find a balance between being kind of being supportive but not being too supportive," she told me. "Because we weren't condoning illegal behaviour."

The economic damage caused by the border blockades was overstated while the protests were underway. In February 2022, cross-border trade actually increased significantly over the previous year as trucks simply diverted to other crossings.[83] Nevertheless it was disruptive and seemed to erode some of the goodwill the convoy had gained from the public, and certain Conservative politicians. On February 10, Bergen once again lauded the convoy for growing into an "international phenomenon" but said "the time has come to take down the barricades, stop the disruptive action, and come together. The economy you want to see reopened is hurting."[84]

All told, the border blockades were a mixed blessing for the truckers. Dichter said he thinks the blockaders were responsible for the ongoing American coverage, particularly from cable news, talk radio, and conservative digital outlets. But Lich said the blockades were "harmful in the long run" because of how the media associated them with the Ottawa convoy organizers, despite the lack of a direct connection. Crucially, the blockades set the stage for unprecedented action from Trudeau's government, bringing the convoy to a sudden end.

PART III

THE EMERGENCY

CHAPTER 10

COURTS, CASH, AND CANS

Money was a great barometer of the convoy's momentum. It was easy to dismiss Twitter's fascination with the truckers as the work of bots, but the millions of dollars pouring into convoy-related fundraising campaigns showed real-world support for what the protesters were doing. Contrary to the speculation and accusations of convoy skeptics in media and politics, the donations were overwhelmingly from individual Canadians, not foreign actors seeking to sow discord in Canadian politics and society. The government's own financial security officials admitted so under oath.[85]

At the same time, money was at the root of most of the convoy's grief. The Freedom Convoy GoFundMe campaign Tamara Lich started was an instant hit, reaching $1 million in just one week. GoFundMe asked Lich and the convoy's hastily assembled financial committee for details about how the money would be distributed. The company presented this as standard practice, not a convoy-specific hurdle. After days of discussions, GoFundMe released $1 million on January 27, which made its way into a personal bank account Lich held at TD on February 2. GoFundMe had more questions before releasing more money. In a February 1 email to Lich, GoFundMe asked her to confirm that funds would only go towards fuel reimbursement rather than food and shelter, and that it would be limited to those "who engage in peaceful and lawful protests." The company asked how much of the initial $1 million had been distributed (the answer was none, because it hadn't yet cleared into Lich's account), whether Lich would be posting an update reiterating that protests should remain peaceful, how many participants would be supported by the second release of funds, and so on. GoFundMe also said it would be "reaching out to local law enforcement to obtain information on the individuals suspected of engaging in illegal activity during the protests."

On February 2, GoFundMe told Lich it was placing the fundraiser "under review," meaning new donations couldn't be accepted because of "reports of potentially unlawful activities by protesters in Ottawa and nonresponse to our multiple requests for assurance that no funds raised on GoFundMe have been or will be transmitted to individuals suspected of acting unlawfully." GoFundMe wanted some form of proof that only those "peacefully and lawfully protesting" would receive any money. The company said its definition of peaceful and lawful meant "no blockades of roads and highways." Justice Centre for Constitutional Freedoms (JCCF) lawyer Eva Chipiuk and Keith Wilson intervened. They had to jump headfirst into the funding fight from the moment they arrived in Ottawa. In a February 3 email, Wilson told GoFundMe, which was sitting on $10 million in convoy donations at the time, that the funds raised would go towards reimbursement costs, that the convoy was a peaceful and lawful protest, and that the convoy was "committed to transparency and accountability." Evidently, the company was not convinced.

On February 4, GoFundMe abruptly cancelled the Freedom Convoy 2022 crowdfunding campaign without giving any notice to Lich, Wilson, or Chipiuk. The campaign was taken offline, and anyone trying to visit it was redirected to a blog post in which the company claimed it had "evidence from law enforcement that the previously peaceful demonstration has become an occupation, with police reports of violence and other unlawful activity." None of this evidence was produced. Organizers have told me they weren't informed of any specifics. Ottawa Mayor Jim Watson admitted that he and the city's police made a "plea" to GoFundMe to kill the campaign.[86]

GoFundMe pledged to redirect the funds raised to "credible and established charities chosen by the Freedom Convoy 2022 organizers and verified by GoFundMe." Backlash was swift, and the next day the company backtracked and agreed to refund donations automatically.[87]

On the same day that GoFundMe axed the fundraiser, TD froze the bank accounts Lich used to receive e-transfers and the initial million dollars from the fundraising campaign. Organizers say this move also came without notice. Lich only learned the account was frozen when she went to a branch to arrange for a wire transfer or bank draft to pay for an airplane charter that Freedom Corp was booking to fly people to Ottawa. TD said it was freezing the money while it investigated where it came from—a curious excuse given GoFundMe did its own due diligence on the $1 million and TD would have quite easily been able to see where the money directly transferred to Lich's account from other donors originated. This was the first of many financial and legal blows the convoy would face.

Also on February 4, Ottawa lawyer Paul Champ served Wilson with a $9.8 million (later increased to $306 million) proposed class action lawsuit against the convoy. The plaintiff was a federal government employee, Zexi Li, although she was representing downtown Ottawa residents generally. Named as defendants were Chris Barber, Benjamin Dichter, Lich, Pat King, and 60 "John Doe" truckers. Alongside the lawsuit was an application for an injunction to end the honking that had altered Ottawa's soundscape, or in Champ's words, caused "significant mental distress and harm." After hearing the case, a judge granted the injunction the following Monday. For ten days (it was later extended), honking air horns or train horns was effectively prohibited in Ottawa. Police had the power to arrest and remove anyone who violated the injunction, which the judge ordered Lich and Barber to share on social media. Conspiracies swirled online suggesting that Li was a Liberal operative or a foreign agent. She was a downtown Ottawa resident genuinely disrupted by the convoy, which made her a good candidate for the suit, given the truckers clearly weren't going anywhere. The injunction was trumpeted as a loss for the convoy, but all the organizers I spoke to said they were secretly grateful for it. The honking was relentless in the convoy's early days. The injunction gave organizers an excuse to tell the truckers they needed to lay off the horns while being able to blame someone else. From then until the end of the convoy, there were few complaints about noise.

* * *

After the GoFundMe debacle, the convoy immediately set up a campaign on the American Christian crowdfunding platform, GiveSendGo. Its website was far less polished than GoFundMe's, but it was committed to the cause and opposed cancel culture as a matter of principle. What happened with GoFundMe became international news, especially in the United States, where the political right was already wary of Big Tech companies using their power to squash conservative voices. GiveSendGo's servers couldn't keep up with the traffic. The website was up and down as the company's tech team tried to keep up with the demand. Donations surged, with some people redirecting their refunded GoFundMe donations and often doubling or tripling them to prove a point. In addition to their stance on vaccine mandates, the truckers were becoming underdogs in a battle against Big Tech and Big Banks. The GiveSendGo campaign reached $10 million in a third of the time it took the GoFundMe campaign to do the same.

Meanwhile, the Ontario government was secretly taking the convoy organizers to court to cut off the funds. On February 10, Ontario's attorney general secured an *ex parte* hearing after which an Ontario Superior Court judge issued a restraint order banning spending or "dealing with, in any manner whatsoever," money donated to GiveSendGo campaigns on behalf of the convoy or Adopt-a-Trucker. The order was binding nationwide. Any Canadian bank account that had touched the affected money was frozen. The American GiveSendGo didn't see it as a problem.

"Know this," a February 10 tweet from GiveSendGo said. "Canada has absolutely ZERO jurisdiction over how we manage our funds here at GiveSendGo."[88]

However confident the company felt, the Ontario court order removed any legal avenue to get the money into Canada. Things got trickier a few days later when Champ filed a secret application for a Mareva injunction, a fraud prevention tool used when there are fears that money will be moved if a defendant is aware of proceedings against them. A judge granted this injunction on February 17, ensnaring the bank accounts and even cryptocurrency wallets of Freedom Corp. and its board members, as well as other organizers and volunteers. Because of the Mareva injunction, more than four million dollars en route to the convoy from the GiveSendGo campaign were frozen with Stripe, a Canadian payment processing company.

Around the same time, a hacker accessed the full donor log for the GiveSendGo campaign, publishing a list of names, emails, addresses and donation amounts for the campaign's donors. Mainstream media outlets started canvassing the list and doxing donors.[89] An Ontario government employee was fired on the spot after a journalist uncovered a $100 donation she made to the convoy and asked Ontario Premier Doug Ford's office about it. (She later launched a lawsuit against her former employer over the dismissal).[90] The leaked data showed there were donations from people outside Canada, but this was unsurprising given how much global media coverage GoFundMe's cancellation of the convoy and the government's targeting of the GiveSendGo money got. The data also demonstrated that many Canadians were inspired by the truckers: some companies gave tens of thousands of dollars. A London, Ontario businessman donated $25,000 US, and when the media tried to shame him for it was all too happy to explain how important it was for him to take a stand against government overreach.[91] "I am not prepared to accept a country without freedom for my family, my children, my friends, my neighbours and every other Canadian," the donor, Holden Rhodes, wrote in a statement to the *London Free Press*.[92]

What GoFundMe, the City of Ottawa, the Ontario government, and the mainstream media didn't get, however, was that money wasn't fuelling the convoy.

Courts, Cash, and Cans

* * *

Truckers were promised reimbursement when they set out to Ottawa, and most of them were made whole by cash donations; others had no expectations but were grateful to receive what funds they did. The interesting development was that most of the things organizers expected they'd have to pay for—food, clothing, facilities—often showed up as in-kind gifts. Also, cash was king in the convoy. "It was insane," Wellington St. block captain David Paisley said. "Slipping people bills, handshakes with bills, Bibles with bills, cards with bills."

There was such generosity that if anyone put out a bucket, it soon would be filled with money. This opened the door to people preying on others' good nature, which happened in at least one widely publicized case of a man who collected thousands from others while claiming to media that he drained his life savings helping others at the convoy.[93]

No one was able to give a precise figure on how much cash changed hands, but it was a lot. Some was handed directly to individual truckers; some was donated (thousands of dollars at a time) to organizers to distribute to truckers. Bulk fuel orders cost thousands of dollars. Trucks being trucks, things broke down and needed to be replaced—this sometimes cost thousands as well. And then there were hotel and equipment costs for the command centres and the main stage, and so on. Most of what was needed was paid for in cash.

Processing cash donations was one of the regular functions at the Swiss Hotel command centre, where Freedom Corp's lead accountant Chad Eros operated. Every dollar in and out of the Swiss was accounted for, but organizers also treated cash like a hot potato. They resisted stashing it at the Swiss for security reasons, and also because of the optics. "It was really like a movie," Lich said. "The cash would come in. There were people that would count it, stuff it in envelopes. We'd stuff it in our pockets in our coats and run out to wherever and try to get as much of it out as we could."

John, the head of fuel distribution, said he recalled one day when over $90,000 was handed out to truckers in envelopes with $500 in each. All the money had come in the form of unexpected cash donations.

It was often the smaller amounts donated that were the most moving. I heard one story of an older woman on a fixed income who handed a random trucker a $10 bill because it was all she could spare that month. Others assembled little toiletry bags which had $5 bills or Tim Hortons gift cards among their contents.

Organizers branched out to cryptocurrency to try to circumvent traditional finance altogether. Apart from cryptocurrencies' volatility, a lot of truckers and even some Freedom Corp board members simply didn't understand how they worked or were inherently distrustful of them. Dichter was a big booster of Bitcoin and actively promoted channels to collect Bitcoin donations for the convoy. A cryptocurrency advocate who goes by the name NobodyCaribou helped distribute to truckers envelopes with detailed instructions on how to access the Bitcoin that had been divvied up for them. Bitcoin's public ledger shows much of this (though not all) was, in fact, accessed by the truckers as intended.[94] The Mareva injunction did include dozens of Bitcoin wallets, although, practically speaking, the court didn't have the technological means to freeze many of them given Bitcoin's decentralized nature.

The Bitcoin example is one of many situations where the convoy found a window when a door was closed. Any time there was a legal or political roadblock in the online fundraising, cash donations would surge. While there was a ton of money—so much that no one could or would give me a number—the money remained a symptom and not a cause of the convoy's momentum. This was a subtle point, but one lost in the media obsession with the money. How much was there? How was it going to be spent? Was an organizer going to run off with it? These were all legitimate questions with eight-figure sums. I asked several of them myself. But the questions did tend to overstate the importance of money to the movement.

* * *

On Sunday, February 6, police raided Coventry, the convoy's staging area and fuel distribution centre that officers had initially helped to set up. Dozens of heavily armed police officers descended on the site in the evening, ten days into the convoy's time in Ottawa, seizing a fuel tanker and removing a handful of vehicles. Snipers overlooked the operation, which was the first overt law enforcement measure the convoy had really encountered.

John, the head of fuel distribution, said he received a tip about the operation through the convoy's police sources, and immediately called for all-hands-on-deck at Coventry. The approach up to that point had been to ration fuel and only distribute the bare minimum that was needed. With an impending raid, there was a new plan. "Release all of it," John told his team. "I don't care what you're doing. Every drop of fuel needs to be in a tank. I don't care about the strategy. I don't care where it goes. You see a tank, it's not filled? Fill it up."

At around 5:00 p.m. that day, John learned one of his fuel volunteers was arrested by police. He made the call to halt fuel delivery.

While he wouldn't stop anyone who wanted to continue fuelling from doing so, he didn't want to put anyone at risk on his orders. But the snap decision proved unnecessary, John said. They had already managed to clear out almost all the fuel they had from Coventry. It was either in trucks or on its way downtown. Police said they seized 3,200 litres of fuel, but according to John, almost none of that was destined for trucks.[95] In Ontario, businesses in industries like farming, construction, and forestry can buy tax-free diesel for use in machinery and off-road vehicles. The fuel is dyed red to distinguish it from the taxed fuel drivers need to use in vehicles operating on public roads. Protesters were using coloured fuel in generators, but not the trucks. Almost all of what police seized was coloured fuel. "The fools got what we couldn't use anyway," John said, with no effort to hide his amusement.

As word got out about the raid, fuel started flooding in. "That very night within two hours, we had doubled the amount that they had seized, but [uncoloured] now so we could use that on the trucks," John said. "Every single time they reacted excessively like that, they shot themselves in the foot and we got double the amount of whatever we had."

The next day, hundreds of people walked around downtown Ottawa with jerrycans, some filled with diesel and others empty just to mess with police officers. There were smaller fuel seizures after that day, but for the most part police backed off and John was able to resume the fuel delivery plan he had in place before the raid.

All told, the convoy was consistently able to supply protesters with the resources they needed to stay on the scene for all three weeks. While fuel required adaptivity, it was never in short supply except in the early days when organizers were still trying to figure things out. Food was never an issue. There was plenty of money to cover expenses, including the bouncy castles and the jumbotron. Try as they might, governments, the courts, and tech companies could only make things somewhat more difficult for the protesters; they could not starve them of money, food, fuel, or enthusiasm.

CHAPTER 11

THE TALKS

Since before the convoy arrived in Ottawa, organizers prided themselves on keeping open lines of communication with law enforcement. A trove of text messages, email records, and phone logs show how frequent the contact became. Convoy organizers had two primary liaisons, one with the Ottawa Police Service and another with the Ontario Provincial Police. The written interactions I've seen between organizers and their liaisons were always cordial, although it's clear through my conversations with organizers that they never quite trusted the police. Chris Barber spoke with officers throughout the journey to Ottawa. Chris Garrah, who had set up Adopt-a-Trucker, did most of the pre-arrival talking with police about plans on the ground in Ottawa. Danny Bulford, the former RCMP officer, stepped in as the organizers' go-between on security matters. By January 30, Tom Marazzo, the former Canadian Armed Forces captain, was also in the mix.

Marazzo had a daily call with the OPP liaison discussing whatever was happening, often revolving around emergency lanes and road closures—an area in which Marazzo took a particular interest as the parent of a child who had spent time in ambulances. Even with Marazzo's daily calls, Bulford continued to speak to police, as did

Tamara Lich. Later on, lawyers Keith Wilson and Eva Chipiuk started taking a more active role in the discussions, especially as the legal stakes heightened. As a result, organizers who weren't always on the same page were having discussions with police from multiple agencies who weren't always on the same page.

The top concern for police and the City of Ottawa was the presence of trucks on residential streets. The convoy never intended to disrupt residential areas, but when downtown filled up or road closures blocked their access, many just parked where they could outside the core.

While the OPP, Royal Canadian Mounted Police, and parliamentary security were all involved, the Ottawa Police Service was the lead agency. The longer the convoy ran, the more Ottawa's police chief, Peter Sloly, faced criticism. Members of the city's police services board took aim at him for not being more aggressive in efforts to expel the convoy. Early on, he conceded the convoy might need a political solution rather than a policing solution, which is precisely what organizers were seeking.[96] Sloly later said the city needed more resources—namely 1,800 additional officers and staff, to manage the scene.[97] Convoy organizers were generally okay with Sloly's handling of their protest, given that it was under his leadership that they were able to take over downtown Ottawa. This also explains why those who wanted the convoy gone were less supportive of Sloly. Marazzo was worried Sloly might resign or get fired, which he suspected would usher in a successor with a drastically different approach. His prediction would eventually come true. "We wanted to take the pressure off of Peter Sloly," Marazzo said. "We knew if we didn't, the police were going to be forced to ratchet up what they were doing."

To do this, Marazzo wanted to take the pressure off the city of Ottawa. One of the big sticking points for police and the city was the cluster of trucks blocking Rideau St. and Sussex Dr., a normally high traffic intersection just east of the Rideau Canal and a few blocks from Parliament Hill. The Rideau Centre shopping mall, which was closed for the entirety of the protest, sits on the northeast and southeast corners of the intersection. The intersection is also near the Chateau Laurier, the American embassy, and the Byward Market district. The problem for both police and convoy organizers was that the truckers who camped out there were a stubborn set. Most of them had arrived on their own and not with any of the organized convoys. When police asked for the intersection to be cleared, Marazzo and Lich were open to it but had trouble getting buy-in from the truckers. Making things easier for Ottawa, as Marazzo wanted, was a tough sell when Ottawa's mayor blasted the convoy as an "aggressive and hateful occupation of our neighbourhoods, which has nothing to do with the truckers' quarrel against vaccine mandates."[98]

Marazzo was invited to a confidential meeting at city hall with Ottawa's city manager, Steve Kanellakos, on February 8. He attended with Wilson and Chipiuk; four Ottawa police and Ontario Provincial Police liaisons were also present. Wilson, Chipiuk, and Marazzo were frisked by police on their way into the meetings and had their phones taken away. They didn't object, but thought that the measure demonstrated the lack of trust in both directions. Wilson said he went in with an olive branch at the ready—a promise to accept a renewal of the horn honking injunction, which was about to expire.

During the meeting, Marazzo and Wilson said they would try to move trucks from residential areas downtown and clear the Rideau and Sussex intersection; police agreed to move their concrete barricades temporarily so that trucks could get onto Wellington St. The caveat, however, which Wilson and Marazzo knew all too well, was that no one could force the truckers to do anything they didn't want to do. "We don't control them," Wilson said. "We don't even know who they are. No one signed up. It's not a curling bonspiel, it's not a golf tournament. We can't say 'Oh no, sorry, this is your tee time sir. You can't tee off from here now.'"

No government—municipal, provincial, or federal—had officially recognized the convoy in any way before this meeting. It was kept quiet because no one wanted what they felt was progress to be derailed by media questioning why the city was legitimizing the convoy, or by convoy supporters questioning why their leaders were selling out. Wilson said they agreed that if anyone learned about the meeting, they would say it was only between convoy leaders and police—no city manager—with city hall chosen only because it was neutral turf. News of the meeting did not leak, which Wilson suspected increased the trust the city and police had for him and the convoy leaders.

Marazzo thought giving up Rideau and Sussex was tactically a bad move because if all the trucks were lined up on one street—Wellington—it would be easier for police to swoop in and remove them. But he also believed something had to give. Wilson and Lich hustled to get the truckers in the intersection on board. Some remained stubborn. Others thought it was a trap and that they and the convoy leaders were getting hoodwinked by police. Yet they somehow got the truckers to agree. Police prepared to bring in the front-end loader to clear the concrete barricades.

The operation was set for the evening of February 10. Wilson and Lich were on site to work with the truckers and police. Again, the convoy's grassroots momentum worked against them. The situation quickly devolved into chaos. A group of demonstrators thought the machine was there to haul away trucks, so they surrounded it. News of the stand-off spread on social media, especially the audio messaging app Zello, prompting an influx of protesters from Parliament Hill. Within half an hour, there were hundreds, if not more than a thousand, people surrounding police and the city's vehicles, singing "O Canada." Wilson advised police that the move just couldn't happen. The protesters cheered as the police left the area single-file. Rideau and Sussex remained blocked until the end of the convoy.

* * *

Around the same time that Marazzo was talking to Ottawa's city manager, another back channel was opening up. Dean French, the former chief of staff to Ontario Premier Doug Ford, was rapt by the convoy. As it went on and he saw increasing tensions between protesters and the City of Ottawa, he saw an opportunity to throw his political contacts and mediation experience into the mix to help reach a resolution. French viewed the convoy leaders as "proud, big-hearted Canadians . . . standing up for a righteous cause."[99] He also had a good relationship with Mayor Jim Watson going back to their time working together while French was running Ford's office. The call for French's help actually came from former Newfoundland premier Brian Peckford, who knows French through conservative circles. Peckford is the last living first minister from when the Charter of Rights and Freedoms was adopted in 1982. Throughout the pandemic, he has been an outspoken critic of governments' abuses of the Charter through mandates and lockdowns. Peckford, unvaccinated against

COVID-19, was also suing the federal government over its vaccine mandate for air travel (he is represented by Wilson and the JCCF). At Peckford's request, French called Watson to see if some form of talks were even on the table to deescalate the situation.

French was worried about someone on little sleep—either a police officer or a trucker—slipping up in some way. The tenser things got, the higher the risk of some sort of explosion. He was banking on both sides getting that.

"Of course he was interested in coming to a resolution," French said of Watson. "Nothing was happening from their end of things in Ottawa."

After learning of Watson's openness, French reached out to Wilson to see if convoy organizers would be willing to sit down. Getting the organizers together was often like herding cats, but Wilson was able to get buy-in from Lich and the Freedom Corp board to at least hear French out. French believed the protesters had a right to be on Wellington St., but not in residential areas. He said he made that clear to both Watson and convoy leaders.

French was not being paid by anyone: he thought he could help and was happy to do so. On February 11, he flew to Ottawa and rented the Renaissance meeting room on the twenty-fourth floor of the Westin. He felt a sense of urgency around his mission: it seemed to him that the runway for a municipal solution was getting shorter. On February 10, news broke that Premier Ford was about to invoke a provincial state of emergency. It was mainly sparked by holdups at the Canada-US border caused by blockades, but such a move by the province would challenge Ottawa's autonomy over the protests. Despite his connection to Ford, French was only negotiating at the municipal level.

During their meeting with French at the Westin, organizers admitted they never intended to be on residential streets, so it wasn't a stretch for them to agree to get the trucks—or at least try to get the trucks—off of them. French was aware of Marazzo's meeting at city hall a couple of days earlier, but knew nothing concrete had come of it, especially after the previous night's aborted attempt to clear Rideau and Sussex. After the meeting, French took things back to Watson's office and returned a couple of hours later with a proposal for Wilson to bring to Lich and the board.

After some back and forth, French, the City of Ottawa, and the convoy organizers agreed that Watson and Lich would put out public letters—first Watson, then Lich a little while later to cloak how choreographed it was. In his letter, published the afternoon of Sunday, February 13, Watson offered to meet with Lich to discuss the protesters' concerns, conditional on the removal of all trucks from residential streets and Coventry, and agreement to not deploy more trucks or protesters in these areas. The letter demanded "clear evidence" of the departure from residential areas by noon on Monday, February 14. "I look forward to your protest movement meaningfully delivering on these steps as a show of goodwill towards our community," Watson wrote. "I hope we can make progress to alleviate the extreme and undue burden this protest, and the occupation of our residential districts in the core and elsewhere, have had on the residents and businesses of downtown Ottawa."

The letter was addressed to Lich as president of Freedom Convoy 2022. This inclusion was a win for Wilson, as it was recognition of the convoy as an entity by a government.

Lich's letter, published shortly after, affirmed the truckers "have always been about peaceful protest." She wrote: "We have made a plan to consolidate our protest efforts around Parliament Hill. We will be working hard over the next 24 hours to get buy-in from the truckers. We hope to start repositioning our trucks on Monday."

By the time the letters were published, the repositioning had actually already begun, with a plan to move forty to fifty trucks on February 12. The first priority was to load up Wellington St. Any trucks that couldn't fit there would go to one of the out-of-town encampments like 88 or Arnprior. Lich distributed a "Freedom Manifest" signed by her and the road captains and Freedom Corp board members. In the document, they suggested consolidation was the best way to ensure the convoy's continued presence in Ottawa. "We need to reposition our trucks so we don't give the Prime Minister the excuse he desperately wants to use force and seize our trucks," the letter said.

Originally, the city wanted the entire relocation done within twenty-four hours, Wilson said, but convoy organizers insisted that it would take at least seventy-two hours. French and Wilson saw the first day of the relocation as a success. There were some hurdles with police not wanting to let trucks through because they hadn't heard about the deal, but things got sorted out without issue. The City of Ottawa seemed pleased as well.

On Sunday, day two, road captains had arranged for dozens more trucks to move, but police blocked them. Unlike the day before, they refused to budge. They said it was only a twenty-four-hour deal, and that was that. A group of police went over to the Swiss Hotel, where Wilson said he "read the Riot Act" to them. After taking a phone call, presumably from a superior, one of the officers apologized and admitted to Wilson they got it wrong and would help with the relocations for the rest of the day. Things chugged along nicely for a few hours until the letters came out.

City News ran a story that Watson and convoy organizers struck a deal. Convoy spokesperson Benjamin Dichter tweeted a link to the video report calling it fake news.[100] "No deal has been struck, the federal government has not yet lifted its mandates and passports," he wrote. "Do not watch #Fakenews, it's bad for your mental health. This is completely false."

Lich retweeted Dichter's post at 8:27 p.m. (nearly five hours after Watson published his letter), adding "The media lies to their viewers. No 'deal' has been made. End the mandates, end the passports. That is why we are here."

Wilson was annoyed by this amateurish, self-induced communications crisis. Part of the problem was the rapid speed at which everything was happening. Also, because of the confidential nature of the back-channel discussions, the plan wasn't known to the larger group of organizers. Dichter wasn't being specifically excluded, but because he was tending to a broken ankle, he was stuck at his own hotel and not in on meetings he might have joined were he more ambulatory. Wilson didn't know why Dichter, who often called in to meetings, wasn't in the loop on the deal with the City of Ottawa. Dichter told me he was also given blatantly wrong information, including that no talks had taken place when, in fact, the message was supposed to be that no one should admit that talks were taking place.

Lich tweeted a correction that evening, acknowledging that there was a deal. In an attempt at saving face over the mix-up, she said that her earlier dismissal of the story was referring to the fact that no deal had been struck with the federal government. Convoy leadership continued to maintain that the feds would have to budge on vaccine mandates and passports for them to even consider a meeting. The deal was widely covered by media and the convoy was on track to finish its relocation the next day. And then Justin Trudeau invoked the Emergencies Act.

CHAPTER 12

THE EMERGENCIES ACT

On Valentine's Day, the convoy was prepared to continue its plan to move all trucks onto Wellington St. or out of Ottawa. Chris Barber posted a TikTok video of he and lawyer Eva Chipiuk working with police to rearrange trucks in fulfillment of the agreement.[101] Meanwhile, Keith Wilson and Tamara Lich were getting ready for a meeting with former Newfoundland premier Brian Peckford, who had flown to Ottawa on a charter (because his vaccination status prohibited him from travelling commercially) from his home in British Columbia. At 79, Peckford had become something of a civil liberties icon among those who appreciated his opposition to vaccine mandates as a stalwart defense of Canadian freedoms.

Lich and Wilson were on their way to the Lord Elgin hotel to meet Peckford when they heard the news: later that day, Prime Minister Justin Trudeau was set to invoke the Emergencies Act for the first time in Canada's history. The federal Emergencies Act was passed in 1988 as a replacement to the War Measures Act, a wartime emergency law that had only ever been used during World War I, World War II, and, controversially, by former prime minister Pierre Trudeau during the October Crisis in 1970. The Emergencies Act was broad, allowing for

119

public welfare and public order emergencies in addition to war emergencies. It also, supposedly, requires compliance with the Charter of Rights and Freedoms, which didn't exist when the War Measures Act was created. But in its thirty-four years lifespan, which includes the 1990 Oka crisis, 9/11, a banking crisis and a global pandemic, no prime minister saw fit to use it. Until Trudeau.

Lich was baffled. "I was shocked that the government would to go to such great lengths for bouncy castles and so much love and peace," she told me. "Because we hadn't done anything, right? So, I was a bit incredulous that they were going to these lengths without even speaking to anyone." When they got to the hotel, Wilson told Peckford the news. "Dear Lord," he replied.

"He understood the gravity of the moment that the prime minister has just invoked the War Measures Act—the modern version of it," Wilson said. "Because there are protesters in Ottawa with jumpy castles and hot tubs and trucks and hot dogs and Canadian flags and Alberta flags and guys with Quebec flags hugging guys with Alberta flags, you know, and singing "O Canada" spontaneously. The horror of it, you know."

Peckford and Lich planned to hold an emergency press conference that afternoon at the Sheraton, before Trudeau had a chance to set the agenda himself. Reading from a prepared speech, Lich was defiant.

"We are not afraid," she said. "In fact, every time the government decides to further defend our civil liberties, our resolve strengthens and the importance of our mission becomes clearer. We will remain peaceful, but planted, on Parliament Hill until the mandates are decisively ended."

* * *

"Here, in our capital city, families and small businesses have been enduring illegal obstruction of their neighbourhoods," Trudeau said. "Occupying streets, harassing people, breaking the law: this is not a peaceful protest."

In his announcement, Trudeau spent more time talking about border blockades than anything happening in Ottawa. While the border blockades were disruptive (and not directed by the Ottawa convoy team) most of them, including the critical Windsor-Detroit crossing, had already been dismantled without the Emergencies Act. Police managed to reopen the bridge connecting Windsor and Detroit in a little over a day on February 12, two days before Trudeau claimed the federal government was needed. The Coutts crossing in Alberta was slower to end, but it was also ultimately cleared without federal emergency powers, and Alberta Premier Jason Kenney vehemently opposed Trudeau's invocation of the Emergencies Act. RCMP Commissioner Brenda Lucki later confirmed before a House of Commons committee that police didn't need the Emergencies Act to deal with border blockades.[102] (The City of Ottawa had declared a state of emergency on February 6, followed by a provincial declaration aimed predominantly at border blockades on February 11.)

Yet Trudeau claimed the situation was so dire it required "additional tools" neither the federal nor provincial governments had without the Emergencies Act. He promised these tools would comply with the Charter of Rights and Freedoms, as the Act requires, and that deep down he supports free expression and the right to protest. But not this protest.

The Emergencies Act has stringent criteria on what constitutes a "public order emergency," which Trudeau's government maintained the convoy had created. A public order emergency exists only when there are pressing "threats to the security of Canada," the Emergencies Act says. These could come in the form of espionage or sabotage; foreign influenced campaigns; activities that threaten, direct or use acts of violence for political goals; or activities seeking violent overthrow of government.[103] Trudeau said the convoy had plans to use "serious violence" for its political goals. He was effectively calling it a terror group.

Trudeau promised the emergency measures would be "time-limited, geographically targeted, as well as reasonable and proportionate to the threats they are meant to address." When they came out, they looked anything but.

The orders gave police the ability to restrict movement in areas the government decided were "critical infrastructure." The government's list included border crossings, and also anywhere COVID-19 vaccines were administered, among other locations. (Not Parliament Hill, oddly). It also empowered the government to conscript unwilling tow truck drivers to remove vehicles—a necessity given that many tow truck operators didn't want to get involved, either out of fear of reprisal or because they supported the convoy. Crucially, the government was also waging financial war on people affiliated with the convoy.

"This is about following the money," Finance Minister Chrystia Freeland said. "This is about stopping the financing of these illegal blockades. We are today serving notice: if your truck is being used in these protests, your corporate accounts will be frozen. The insurance on your vehicle will be suspended."

Freeland had spent the weekend meeting with CEOs of Canadian banks soliciting ideas on what to do about the convoy. Under the emergency order, banks could immediately freeze or suspend an account without a court order if they suspected it was connected to the convoy. Banks would be protected from any civil liability, meaning there'd be no recourse if your account was frozen.

Trudeau called this a "last resort," which organizers found incredulous given the federal government hadn't so much as sent an intern to speak with them. Whether discussions would have been productive or not is unknown, but the government never tried, so it was difficult to claim all other options were exhausted.

Wilson believed the federal government saw that its window of opportunity was closing with the City of Ottawa and convoy organizers working together to move trucks to Wellington, which would have concentrated the pressure on the federal government. "They wanted to invoke the Emergencies Act and they needed a pretense," Wilson suggested.

The government claimed there was an explicitly violent nature to the protests. This was not just for the politics of the situation, but, crucially, to ensure the Emergencies Act had a legal basis. This claim was slightly easier to make following arrests that had been made in Coutts, Alberta. On February 14, police seized a cache of long guns, handguns, body armour, and ammunition and charged four people with conspiracy to murder.[104] Police claimed the four men planned to kill RCMP officers, although at the time of writing, little information is available about the alleged plot. The federal government tried to link the group in Coutts to the protest in Ottawa. "Several of the individuals at Coutts have strong ties to a far-right extreme organization with leaders who are in Ottawa," public safety minister Marco Mendicino said on February 16. "We're talking about a group that is organized, agile, knowledgeable and driven by an extremist ideology where might makes right, and this is completely contrary to our democratic values."

Reporters pushed Mendicino for details about the nature of the group and plot he alluded to. He replied that it was a "sophisticated and capable organization of a small number of individuals" with the goal of overthrowing the government. Asked specifically who he was referring to, Mendicino told a reporter they were "very good questions for law enforcement."

Pressed further, Mendicino backtracked to a position that was unrecognizable to his initial claim. "The rhetoric that supported the movement in Coutts is very similar, strikingly similar, to the kind of rhetoric that we're seeing not only in Ottawa but right across the country," he said.

"It sounds like you are making the connection between the rhetoric of suspects who are accused of conspiring to attempt murder in Coutts, Alberta and the organizers here," another reporter said. "Is that what your conclusion is or is that something that's backed up by evidence of an ongoing law enforcement investigation?"

"No, I think you have it right," Mendicino conceded. "The pattern that we're seeing here is in the rhetoric that is being used not only in Coutts, not only in Ottawa, but right across the country."

The activist group Canadian Anti-Hate Network suggested the group Mendicino was referring to was Diagolon, an online community created by Canadian Armed Forces veteran and online streamer Jeremy MacKenzie, built around a fictitious country.[105] Photos shared by the RCMP of the Coutts weapons seizures showed body armour with shoulder patches of Diagolon's "flag," a black rectangle with a diagonal white line through it.

"It's a meme," MacKenzie said in a video. "There is no army. There is no militia. There are no terrorists. There are no weapons caches. There are no threats, no organizations, no planning."[106] He said the patches are available for anyone to purchase and their presence cannot be used to infer his or Diagolon's involvement in anything violent, though he also dismissed the weapons seizure and arrests as a "false flag" operation.

* * *

Most of the convoy leaders were holed up in their war room at the Sheraton watching Trudeau announce the new measures in a televised press conference. Their emotions varied. Trudeau was taking these extraordinary steps because of them. One person told me they had an odd sense of pride about it, if only because the reason for the trip to Ottawa in the first place had been to send a message and this showed it was received. Lich couldn't believe it was necessary. Security lead Danny Bulford was unsurprised because it just proved his sense that Canada was seeing an "ever increasing movement towards authoritarian governance." Spokesperson Benjamin Dichter said he was "confused." He figured it meant an end to the protest, but also thought it would spectacularly backfire on Trudeau, especially with rumblings that some of his caucus members weren't thrilled with his handling of the pandemic. Wilson feared the Emergencies Act could usher in a "Tiananmen Square moment" for Canada. "I felt that police were going to resort to violence," he said. "That was my main thought."

But when he read the emergency proclamation later on, Wilson saw that it specifically said people were allowed to peacefully and lawfully assemble. The emergency proclamation was clear that a public assembly was only illegal if you were seriously disrupting trade or critical infrastructure or supporting the threat or use of "serious violence" against people and property. Wilson knew the order was meant to go after the convoy, but at face value it didn't look like it even applied to them. "I didn't know anybody who was going to do any of those things," he said. "That meant they were allowed to be in Ottawa. The order didn't prevent them."

Ottawa police chief Peter Sloly resigned the day after the Emergencies Act was invoked. Steve Bell, a deputy police chief, was promoted to interim chief. On Thursday, February 16, Bell warned that anyone travelling to "unlawful protest sites to participate in or support the unlawful demonstration can be charged."[107] The Justice Centre for Constitutional Freedoms sent him and the Ottawa Police Service a cease-and-desist letter the next day, warning they had "no authority whatsoever to make such an order," even under the Emergencies Act. Ottawa police never responded. (Wilson said he wasn't expecting them to change their minds, but he had to at least put them on notice).

As Freeland promised, the government and banks started going after people's finances. On February 17, some organizers noticed their accounts—chequing, savings, credit cards, lines of credit, you name it—were frozen. No one knew how wide the net would be, especially with the leaked GiveSendGo donor list circulating. People who donated tiny amounts but were in no way organizers told me they feared their accounts would be frozen. Donors to my show on True North were similarly concerned that a broad assault on any conservative financing was imminent. Everyone knew someone who knew someone whose account was frozen after donating $50 or some such. Many of these stories didn't pan out, but the law certainly had a chilling effect.

Everyone on Freedom Corp's board had their accounts frozen. Their names and addresses were publicly available through the not-for-profit's corporate registration. Tom Marazzo said even his joint account with his wife, who had nothing to do with the convoy, was frozen. The same was true of road captain Sean Tiessen and his wife. A disclosure document filed by the RCMP in court offered a glimpse into how police assembled the information that was passed to banks to pull the trigger on account freezes. One officer's contribution contained photos and biographical details of convoy organizers and activists gleaned from a CTV "guide to the major players in the trucker convoy protest."[108] Other sections of the document were populated by vehicle record searches police conducted from license plate numbers they saw in their patrols in Ottawa.

* * *

Politically, Justin Trudeau appeared to have overplayed his hand with the Emergencies Act. Public opinion showed a majority opposed to the convoy's prolonged presence in Ottawa, but for many Canadians, the invocation of the Emergencies Act vindicated the protesters, who'd been sounding the alarm about government overreach for more than two weeks. A Mainstreet Research poll found that more Canadians were opposed to the emergency measures than were for them, though to be fair there were still large numbers of Canadians in favour.[109] Even lawyer Paul Champ, who filed the proposed class action against the convoy and secured the horn-honking injunction, said that the Emergencies Act was a "dangerous tool that was not required" to deal with the truckers.[110] One of the rules of the Emergencies Act is that Parliament must vote to affirm an emergency within a week of the act's invocation. Trudeau had a minority government, so another party would have to support the Liberals. Trudeau said in his remarks that the vote on the Emergencies Act would be a vote of confidence in his government, an unsubtle signal to the opposition parties that if they didn't want an election, they had better fall in line. The New Democrats did. In 1970, they vociferously opposed Pierre Trudeau's invocation of the War Measures Act, but this was a different NDP.

NDP leader Jagmeet Singh, whose party has often been directly linked to protest movements, struggled to explain how the government was justified to clamp down on this protest, but not others: "Indigenous land defenders, climate change activists, workers fighting for fairness, and any Canadian using their voice to peacefully demand justice should never be subject to the Emergencies Act," he said. But the trucker protest was different because it was "fed on disinformation" with a goal to "disrupt our democracy," he maintained.[111]

The confidence motion ploy was also, it seemed, necessary to keep Trudeau's own Liberal caucus in line. MP Nathaniel Erskine-Smith gave a speech laying out a litany of concerns with the act's invocation, ending with a concession that he has "no interest in an election at this time" so he was voting with Trudeau.[112] The Conservatives were forcefully against the Emergencies Act, as were the Bloc Quebecois, who didn't like the precedent of the federal government mucking around in provincial affairs. With the NDP's support, it was a done deal. Trudeau's "emergency" was endorsed by the House of Commons, although the vote didn't happen until the convoy had already been forced out of Ottawa.

Opposition from civil society groups was robust. On February 17, the Canadian Civil Liberties Association announced it would fight the Emergencies Act in court. "The federal government did not meet the high burden necessary to invoke the Emergencies Act," CCLA executive director Noa Mendelsohn Aviv said.[113] The CCLA took the view that protests are sometimes meant to be disruptive, and that a protest can be both disruptive and nonviolent, or disruptive and lawful. The emergency orders were supposed to be narrow, but actually extended to anywhere in the country if the government decided it wanted to treat a particular protest as unlawful. "They place unprecedented restrictions on every single Canadian's constitutional rights," the CCLA said.

The same day, the Canadian Constitution Foundation announced its own legal challenge, aimed at how the government simply didn't meet the high bar set out by the Emergencies Act for invoking the act.[114] Alberta Premier Jason Kenney's government initially planned to file its own legal challenge, but later opted to join the CCLA and CCF cases as an intervener.[115]

At a press conference, Trudeau insisted nothing about the Emergencies Act would trample on civil liberties or the right to free expression. "We're not using the Emergencies Act to call in the military. We're not suspending fundamental rights or overriding the Charter of Rights and Freedoms. We are not limiting people's freedom of speech. We are not limiting freedom of peaceful assembly. We are not preventing people from exercising their right to protest legally," he said.

Those words did not reflect what was about to happen on the ground.

CHAPTER 13

THE TAKEDOWN

When I arrived back in Ottawa on Thursday, February 17, the mood was markedly different from my previous visit. The Emergencies Act was in play, although no one seemed to know what its implementation would look like beyond extra police officers and tow trucks. Protesters still had the cheery disposition they'd maintained throughout their three weeks in Ottawa—the bouncy castles were still bouncing and the hot tub still steaming—but it was clear organizers knew their time was almost up. Police were locking down the city in real time. Officers canvassed hotels, trucks, and other convoy gathering places handing out copies of a full-page "Notice to Demonstrators" telling everyone to scram or risk arrest. An Ottawa police media release warned that people would encounter police checkpoints and have to "show proof of exemption" if they were travelling into the secure area, despite Justin Trudeau's insistence that civil liberties would be protected.

One of the convoy's key strengths was its numbers. Organizers were looking ahead to the Feb. 19-21 Family Day long weekend in Ontario, expecting an unusually powerful surge of supporters. The challenge was that police were blocking entry to the red zone and no one knew how many day-trippers would be able to make it downtown. "If we can get to Saturday, we've bought ourselves until Tuesday," block captain David Paisley told me Thursday morning.

As the convoy and police saw during the aborted attempt at moving trucks off Rideau and Sussex the week before, it's hard to clear the streets when protesters outnumber police. This time, however, police were mostly successful at blocking entry into the city. They shut down the highway off ramps and main thoroughfares. There were, however, some holes in the perimeter, mostly side streets, which convoy supporters were quietly sharing in group chats to help guide reinforcements into the city.

My visit to Ottawa as a journalist was legal, but there was no guarantee an individual police officer would see it that way. I managed to get downtown before many of the 100 checkpoints were established. Organizers I spoke to had an increasingly warlike mentality. They were not just talking about the convoy's positive energy, but about tactics and strategy. "Hold the line," had become a mantra for organizers and protesters alike.

Police were in the Sheraton lobby when I checked in, handing out notices and fending off appeals from some demonstrators to lay down their badges and switch sides. Among the officers were the two designated Ottawa Police Service liaisons who had been in constant communication with convoy organizers. That relationship had hit the skids when the Emergencies Act came into play: organizers felt the City of Ottawa and Ottawa police no longer had any real authority. Whether or not that was the case, the police were about to make their first big move of the weekend.

That Thursday afternoon, organizer Chris Barber was arrested. He was walking around with other demonstrators when officers approached him. He made small talk with them while he was handcuffed and they emptied his pockets. His two instructions to the person filming the arrest were "call my wife" and "put this on social media right away." (They did both, although I'm not sure in which order). Barber was placed in a police car and driven away, later to be charged with a host of criminal offenses: counselling to commit mischief, counselling to disobey a court order, counselling to obstruct police, and mischief that interferes with the use and enjoyment of property.

As Barber seemed to want, video of the arrest spread rapidly around the convoy camps in Ottawa, especially on Wellington St. "They're coming for us all now," one protester told me.

"Hold the line," one group near the flatbed stage in front of Parliament Hill started chanting.

Lich was at the Swiss Hotel when she learned of Barber's arrest. She knew she was next and didn't want to give police an excuse to go into their command centre. She was with Freedom Corp board member Sean Tiessen, security lead and former RCMP officer Bulford, and John, the head of fuel distribution. They decided to "make ourselves available" to police, Lich said. (In case police did raid the Swiss, volunteers cleared out all the computers, maps, and other physical evidence from the Swiss, "just like in the movies").

The four left the Swiss together. Somewhat naively, Lich walked over to a couple of police officers she encountered and introduced herself and asked if they were looking for her. They were a bit confused by the question and said no. She let them know she'd be up on Parliament Hill if anything changed. Lich said she wanted to spend the time she had left surrounded by the people whose stories and passion had brought her to tears hundreds of times over the past few weeks. When she got to Wellington St. she was treated with the usual fanfare. She even did an impromptu scrum with mainstream media reporters about Barber's arrest.

"It's not an illegal protest, it's in our Charter of Rights and Freedoms," Lich said. Asked what her response will be if she got arrested, Lich proclaimed, "Hold the line!" before walking away from the media as her supporters chanted "Freedom!"[116]

Lich continued walking the streets with her crew, but it wasn't long before a police officer politely approached her. "Ms. Lich," the officer said, "can I talk to you over here for a second?" She joked with her team while the officer handcuffed her and emptied her pockets. Bulford demanded they arrest him, too, but they didn't take him up on the offer immediately (they did arrest him the next day, but released him without charges soon after). As Lich was being walked away in handcuffs, Tiessen shouted "Hold the line!" Instinctively, Lich repeated it, a moment that would later be misrepresented as some sort of call to arms rather than the now familiar rallying cry of the convoy.

Lich had predicted her arrest the night before. She did a teary live stream in which she spoke about the convoy as though it was already over, calling it a "crazy ride" and thanking everyone for their support. "There's a pretty good chance—I think it's inevitable at this point—that I'll probably be going somewhere tomorrow where I'll be getting three square meals a day," she said. "And that's okay. I'm okay with that. And I want you to know that I'm not afraid. I'll probably get some sleep finally."

She asked people to "stay peaceful and please take care of each other," and urged her followers to show love and pray for their opponents in government and the media.

"There will be a tomorrow, and we will get through this," she said.

* * *

None of the organizers knew which of them would be arrested. Beyond Lich and Barber, the highest profile was Benjamin Dichter, who had already tweeted that he had left Ottawa.[117] He later told me he was actually still in Ottawa but had left downtown. Dichter was heavily criticized by a lot of convoy supporters, who saw the retreat as cowardice. Dichter said the convoy's legal team told him to leave.

"You're the only one left who can kind of speak . . . on the issue, because Chris is in jail, Tamara is in jail," Dichter recalled the lawyers telling him. "You need to go. Get out of here." He also hoped it would prove to police that he and other remaining organizers, road captains, and protesters were committed to a peaceful withdrawal.

Keith Wilson and Eva Chipiuk didn't think police would be so brazen as to arrest the lawyers representing the convoy, but they weren't sure. Before her arrest, Lich urged Wilson to find a location no one knew about and hunker down there if things went sideways. Once Barber was arrested, Wilson and Chipiuk got out of the red zone and found another boutique hotel, seemingly one of the few that hadn't played at least some role in any of the convoy's activities.

The lawyers prepared themselves and convoy organizers for this. The Justice Centre for Constitutional Freedoms set up a 1-800 number that all the convoy's leaders could call if they were arrested. The number would connect callers to one in a rotation of criminal lawyers on standby. If one wasn't available, it would go to the next. Wilson said the lawyers also instructed everyone on how to get arrested, advising them to sit cross-legged, put their arms behind their backs and keep their heads down to "avoid getting beat up."

Despite the preparations, Wilson was holding out hope it would all be for nothing—that the right to peaceful protest would prevail. Even after Barber's and Lich's arrests, the protesters carried on as they always had. During a blizzard, no less. Volunteers in the main mess tent on Wellington St. were frying buffalo chicken wings for dinner. Nearby, a couple dozen people danced to House of Pain's "Jump Around." It was not clear that any of them knew it would be their last dance.

* * *

On Friday morning, police started moving in on the trucks and protesters. Because of the expected police action, the House of Commons cancelled its scheduled sitting. This was particularly egregious given the topic on the agenda was debate over the Emergencies Act. In the convoy's three weeks in Ottawa, members of parliament had come and gone with little issue. Some avoided engaging with the protesters, but there were never any reported safety issues. Conservative MP Cheryl Gallant stopped to do an interview with a protester at one point a week earlier and joked about the mood on the ground compared to the media's portrayal of it. "I was expecting a siege and pitchforks and torches, but I'm hearing music and I'm seeing families walk up and down," Gallant said. "It's kind of festive, and actually I'd encourage more Canadians to come down."[118] The first time the House of Commons had to cancel a sitting was because of police action, not anything the protesters were doing.

The enlarged police presence materialized on Rideau St., near the Westin hotel a few blocks east of Parliament Hill. Police stood shoulder-to-shoulder spanning the entire street, right up to the buildings on either side. For the most part, they just stood there. Every ten to fifteen minutes they would move forward, shouting, "Move! Move! Move!" They only seemed to advance six to eight feet at a time. It was glacial. Most people complied, although some resisted. There were a small number of arrests—police would pull someone behind their line and officers taking up the rear would zip tie the person's wrists and put them in a police car that would then take them off-site. As word travelled of the advance, protesters started moving from Wellington St. toward the police line in large numbers. At a certain point, the police cordon was moving so slowly there was concern among protesters that it had to be a distraction for some larger police operation on Wellington (it wasn't). By mid-afternoon, police had only managed to advance a few hundred meters, but they had pushed the protest around the intersection onto Rideau, which turns into Wellington. This would prove critical for what came next.

When the Rideau Canal is frozen, as it was in February, getting in and out of downtown is not particularly difficult. Even with the police line, people were able to sneak around by crossing the canal or cutting through Major's Hill Park behind the Chateau Laurier hotel. In the early afternoon, the police pace suggested it would take hours for them to get to the main convoy site on Wellington, if they could even get there before dusk. I left the police line for a bit in the afternoon. When I returned shortly before 5:00 p.m., cops had pushed protesters west on Rideau St. to the eastern edge of the Chateau Laurier. In my absence, they had picked up the pace, although I didn't realize just how much.

I was off to the side, leaning against the columns in front of the Chateau Laurier's laneway where a reporter I knew and some photojournalists were camped out. I picked the location because I was close enough to the line to get some good video and streaming footage, but not so close that I was interfering with what police were doing. (Several of the mainstream media camera crews were right up at the front line). All morning, as police moved forward, I moved backward.

Suddenly I heard a commotion and screams coming from the middle of the street. I looked over and saw that police on horseback had lurched forward into the crowd, breaking what had been a straight front-line formation. I didn't know it at the time, but the police horses knocked over two demonstrators, including an Indigenous grandmother with a walker. I can't say for certain, but having seen how police had operated all morning and how they were at this point, it looked like a mistake. Police claimed the horses responded to someone throwing a bicycle at them, although no bicycle is visible in any of the footage that's circulated of the incident.[119]

Some of the police aggressively advanced toward the area where I and others were standing, effectively pinning us against the front of Chateau Laurier's concrete portico. But we were still a fair distance from the front line. Seconds later, my face felt wet. My immediate instinct was that someone had thrown water at me, but an instant later, the burning sensation said otherwise. The left side of my face was on fire. I'd been pepper sprayed. A photo captured by a journalist moments later shows me hunched over in disbelief. A woman kindly offered to dump some of her water bottle on my face. It didn't help. Being a journalist (and a millennial), I immediately snapped a selfie and tweeted it out, squinting, with both eyes affected, to see what I was typing.

I wasn't the only journalist assailed by police. New York photojournalist Alex Kent said he was zip tied, put in a "choke hold," and detained for "mischief" while shooting the police activity. It took thirty minutes for his editor to negotiate a release. Rebel News' Alexandra Lavoie was filming near the front line when she was shot in the leg with some sort of gas canister. Ottawa police were seemingly unrepentant, telling media to "keep a distance" unless they want to be "subject to arrest."[120]

There were hundreds of protesters in front of the Chateau Laurier as this stand-off took place, although many of them started to disperse when they realized that horses and pepper spray were in the mix. One woman cried in disbelief that "this was happening in my country." A lot of protesters genuinely believed police were on their side. One speaker from the flatbed stage urged police through the public address system to "remember your oath" as the cops neared. Some frontline officers were supportive, at least privately, of the convoy, but that wasn't going to keep them from their duty. (That said, one of my police contacts who had been feeding me information during the convoy said a few officers called in sick that weekend because they "couldn't do it.")

When I finally left the site to go back to my hotel to properly try to rinse my eyes, I passed a seventy-something woman with a walker at the edge of the Wellington St. encampment. She mistook me for a protester: "I'm holding the line here dear, but they need more people over on Metcalfe St," she told me. I don't know how she fared against the thousands of police, but I had to admire the spirit.

Protesters tried to fortify their position to make it more difficult for police to advance. They moved the wooden police road barricades and spare tires and encased them in snow. At one point, you couldn't go west on Wellington St. towards Parliament Hill without climbing one of these snow banks, although someone later opened up a small corridor. People grabbed any snow shovels they could find and joined the effort. It achieved little. By Friday evening, police had contained the protest to just a few blocks of Wellington St., and their conscripted tow truck drivers quickly pulled trucks out of all the newly secured areas and drove them to an impound lot.

A strange subplot emerged the day of the big Wellington St. crackdown. The *New York Times* mentioned in a tweet and a story that police "arrested demonstrators at gunpoint."[121] Canadian journalists pounced on the claim as sensationalistic and inaccurate. CBC's Carol Off sniped that they should "try a bit harder to get the story right." CBC's Ginella Massa called it "false and incredibly dangerous rhetoric." Global News race journalist Ahmar Khan said the claim "harms journalism," and so on. Some people cancelled their subscriptions to the *Times* over it.

It was a bizarre fight to pick, considering there were photos of police with guns drawn as they made arrests, including a widely circulated photo of police pointing their rifles into a camper they were trying to clear and remove. David Paisley, the block captain and live streamer, said he was personally arrested at gunpoint inside his infamous broadcast shed. He was running his live stream at the time: the cameras were streaming what was happening outside, although the audio of his arrest was broadcast.[122] The *New York Times* later capitulated to the mob and scrapped the "gunpoint" line from its story, though it was accurate, and bizarre how many people pretended otherwise.

* * *

In some ways, Saturday morning was more subdued. Older protesters and those with young families seemed to realize it wasn't a stable environment, so they mostly steered clear, either leaving Ottawa altogether or remaining far from the front lines. Many of the weekend day-trippers were turned away by police. Some parked several kilometres away and hiked in. The police perimeter had gaps but was generally strong. On Friday night, a large pickup truck decked out in flags and camo decals rolled up to my hotel. I chatted with the driver, a French Canadian, and asked how he managed to get through the police perimeter. He seemed confused by the question. "I just took different streets," he said nonchalantly.

I left the red zone to go to the hospital Friday night because of the pepper spraying (a telehealth nurse informed me that if symptoms didn't abate within a couple of hours, I should get checked out). Police didn't stop the taxi I was in when I returned to the red zone at about 3:00 a.m. Saturday morning.

The House of Commons resumed Saturday with members of parliament and staffers locked in the building and heavy security guarding the entrances. Overnight, police had managed to secure most of Wellington St. and, using tow truck operators conscripted into duty under the Emergencies Act, remove dozens of trucks. In numerous photos, company logos are covered up and the tow truck drivers are wearing full face masks to remain anonymous.

Having pushed protesters west on Friday, police were trying to move them south on Saturday. There were concerns that police were doing what's called kettling, a controversial crowd control tactic in which police confine demonstrators to one particular area to either corral them out or trap them and make mass arrests. By early afternoon, police had managed to force protesters one block south of Wellington, to the pedestrian-only Sparks St. Just as soon as they'd secured a section, city crews would come in and erect fencing.

One of the last remaining organizers in Ottawa, Tom Marazzo, called a press conference for 1:00 p.m. at the Lord Elgin. He notified a police contact and asked that no one be denied access to it because he was going to call for a peaceful withdrawal from Ottawa. Marazzo stressed the perennial theme that the convoy is a grassroots movement without a single leader. He expressed uncertainty that Canadian democracy could survive the abuse of power. "The violence came to us when the police arrived," he said. "The police brought the violence. To that end, as a movement, we have chosen to peacefully withdraw from the streets of Ottawa. There is nothing to be gained by being brutalized by police."

Marazzo called on police to remove the barricades so that the remaining truckers could drive out. It was a similar request to one he had made to his OPP contact in a text exchange. The officer replied that truckers should instead leave their vehicles unlocked so they could be cleared without windows being broken.

Marazzo conceded that he couldn't force the truckers to leave Ottawa, but hoped they would to avoid further harm at the hands of police. It was a difficult message to square with "hold the line," which had been proclaimed with increasing frequency by organizers and protesters alike that weekend. He told me there was "no value whatsoever in being used as a human punching bag for police." When police adopted aggressive tactics, the stakes were raised to such an extent that not asking the protesters to leave would be putting them in harm's way, and that would fly in the face of the convoy's nonviolent, peaceful spirit.

Dichter saw Marazzo's withdrawal conference as gratuitous and too late to be of any use. He said his own message a day earlier achieved the same purpose, and that by the time Marazzo took the lectern at the Lord Elgin, everyone had already left or been arrested. "Again, another press conference not authorized by any of us," Dichter said. "For fuck's sake, they keep doing it. It's over and they're still doing it."

Lich was still behind bars while all this was happening. It was only later she was able to catch up on all the news about how police cracked down. "I just burst into tears," Lich said of seeing the footage, particularly of the horse trampling incident. "I said 'How can they do this? How can they do this to their own people?'"

CHAPTER 14

THE AFTERMATH

By Sunday morning, police had reclaimed Ottawa from the convoy. Overnight, fencing had been installed all the way along Sparks St., with police maintaining a hard perimeter around Parliament Hill that you could only get through at a couple of heavily guarded entry points. Police patrolled the streets outside the perimeter, threatening to arrest anyone not walking away from Parliament Hill. Under the letter of the law, even with the Emergencies Act, there was no prohibition against lawful activity or assembly, but police didn't seem to care. I had limited success getting around to document the aftermath of what a couple of people glibly called the 'Battle of Wellington.' At one point on Albert St., I was turned back to my hotel and threatened with arrest because I didn't have a Parliamentary Press Gallery identification badge, which is not a universal press credential but one specific to those reporting on the day-to-day business of Parliament Hill. At another checkpoint, the police officer let me through when I showed him my Twitter profile to demonstrate that I was reporting on the convoy. ("Oh, you're even verified," he said).

Journalists were technically able to access Wellington St. through one of the police gates, though here too I was denied entry for lack of a parliamentary press badge, despite providing identification and a letter of assignment from my editor. At another gate a couple of hundred metres away, my credentials were accepted. These stories reveal how wildly enforcement varied depending on which officer you encountered. Ottawa police reminded people that the "Secured Area remains in effect," boasting about arresting two people for having the audacity to walk around without "proof of exclusion." As Conservative member of parliament Melissa Lantsman pointed out, Canadians were being denied the right to go to Parliament Hill to protest the Emergencies Act.[123] The police force's Twitter account threatened to "actively look to identify" anyone who was involved in the protest and "follow up with financial sanctions and criminal charges."[124]

One woman posted a video of a police officer yelling at her to leave, even grabbing or hitting her camera when he realized she was filming him. Setting aside the civil liberties implications, the strategy got Ottawa police the results they wanted: the protesters went home. My hotel, the Sheraton, was at 100 percent capacity for much of the convoy's time in Ottawa; it dropped to a fraction of that Sunday night as people left the city.

Inside the secure zone, things felt apocalyptic. The only people allowed within its perimeter were police and a handful of journalists. There were no horns or diesel engines and few people. I could hear the snow crunch with every step I took—it definitely wasn't the convoy's city anymore. In my walk around, I happened upon a group of Toronto police officers using their surveillance drone to take a selfie in front of the Parliament buildings. Throughout the morning, police that had come from other jurisdictions left, including the Toronto Police Service's horseback unit. Eventually, the perimeter fencing came down as well, although Wellington has continued to be closed to vehicle traffic, perhaps permanently.

* * *

If there ever had been a national emergency in Ottawa, there wasn't one anymore. Yet parliament had yet had to vote on Trudeau's invocation of the Emergencies Act. On February 21, convoy spokespeople Dagny Pawlak and Benjamin Dichter published an "open letter to Parliament" asking politicians to "carefully reflect upon the historical precedent they are about to set." It didn't matter. Because of Trudeau's insistence that the invocation was a confidence motion, his own caucus and the NDP fell in line and the emergency was upheld—two days after the last trucks were cleared. Trudeau was silent about when he would rescind the emergency declaration. He defended its invocation and teased that an end might be coming soon, but offered nothing concrete. One possible reason it remained in place was so the government and banks could continue to freeze bank accounts as they worked through their information about who was in Ottawa protesting.

All told, police arrested 191 people and laid 391 charges in Ottawa that weekend in connection with their takedown of the convoy. Many protesters were driven to the outskirts of the city and released, though others were charged with offences including obstructing police, mischief, and assaulting a police office.

Police said they seized 115 vehicles. They published online instructions on how someone whose car or truck was towed away could reclaim it. Protesters weren't allowed to retrieve their vehicles from the Ottawa impound lot for at least a week. The cost to retrieve a truck was $1,191, or $516 for a light vehicle. Numerous protesters reported smashed windows and other vehicle damage, even those who said they specifically left doors unlocked and keys in the ignition when they vacated shortly before police moved in.

Ultimately, more than 200 bank accounts, containing a combined $7.8 million, were frozen, the government said.[125] Most, if not all, of the freezes were released in the week following the end of the protest. Some organizers have shared with me that their credit scores took hits and one has reported being turned down when trying to open a new bank account afterwards.

Even after the Emergencies Act freezes were lifted, Freedom Convoy funds remained frozen. The $1.4 million TD secured in early February was transferred into an escrow account, along with over four million dollars from GiveSendGo that was trapped at Stripe after the Mareva injunction. This money will sit in escrow pending the outcome of the proposed class action lawsuit filed against the truckers by lawyer Paul Champ. If the suit is successful, the money could end up going to Ottawa residents.[126] GiveSendGo held firm for a while, but in March threw in the towel and refunded donations, seeing no way to guarantee the government wouldn't get its hands on the money otherwise.[127] An April 7 CBC story claimed that $8 million in convoy donations are "unaccounted for," although this was the money GiveSendGo was in the process of returning to donors.[128]

Chris Barber was released on bail the day after he was arrested, with instructions to leave Ottawa within twenty-four hours and Ontario within five days. Under his bail conditions, he wasn't allowed to directly or indirectly support the convoy. Pat King was arrested and, at the time I'm writing this, remains behind bars with no release in sight and no trial date set.

Tamara Lich was held over the weekend and didn't get a bail hearing until Tuesday, February 22, after which the judge denied her application and kept her in jail. Lich was eventually released on March 7 after another judge reviewed her bail application, but the Metis grandmother nonetheless spent eighteen days behind bars. She was released on conditions that lawyer Keith Wilson said "would likely make Putin envious."

Lich was barred from speaking to Barber, Dichter, Tom Marazzo, Danny Bulford, and several others (some of whom she had never met). She was also given a blanket social media ban, which involved giving her bail surety access to her devices to check periodically that she obeyed. The judge also ordered Lich to not engage in "organization or promotion of anti-COVID-19 mandate activities and Freedom Convoy activities" or support anything related to the Freedom Convoy "verbally, in writing, financially, or by any other means." The crown even tried to have her bail reviewed again to send her back to jail. All the opposition heaped onto Lich by the state and the court only seemed to enhance her appeal among her supporters.

When she got back to her hometown of Medicine Hat, Alberta, she received a hero's welcome. She made sure to express no support of anything convoy-related, but people in the city cheered for her, hugged her, and took photos with her. The Justice Centre for Constitutional Freedoms decided to award her its coveted George Jonas Freedom Award for her unflinching defense of liberty throughout the convoy.

* * *

Under the Emergencies Act, the federal government was required to call a public inquiry into its actions, including the decision to invoke the act and what it did when the act was in force. Trudeau triggered this on April 25, appointing Ontario judge Paul Rouleau to spearhead the inquiry, which must table a report by February 20, 2023. Trudeau's announcement of the inquiry made it seem like he wanted it to look more at the protesters' conduct than the government's: "The Commission will examine the circumstances that led to the declaration being issued and the measures taken in response to the emergency," a statement from Trudeau's office said.[129] "This includes the evolution of the convoy, the impact of funding and disinformation, the economic impact, and efforts of police and other responders prior to and after the declaration."

It didn't bode well for transparency that Trudeau wouldn't commit to allowing the inquiry to have access to confidential cabinet documents, which would reveal discussions and deliberations that took place at the cabinet table, including what, if any, evidence it had to justify the emergency declaration.

None of the organizers I spoke to expressed regret about what happened, except for little things they might have changed with the benefit of hindsight (especially on the media relations and messaging). Some have not wanted to move on from the convoy. Wellington St. block captain David Paisley has continued telling the convoy's stories through his Live From The Shed streams, with occasional broadcasts from the road at some of the many freedom rallies across Ontario scheduled in the weeks and months following the convoy. In April, a group of bikers arranged the "Rolling Thunder" convoy to Ottawa, which was smaller and markedly less celebratory than the Freedom Convoy. Unsurprisingly, it met a much frostier reception from local police.

All the convoy organizers are tremendously proud of their work, and have forged lifelong friendships with others they met in Ottawa.

"I would do it again in a heartbeat," Marazzo told me. "This time, I would just do it better."

Dichter said he regretted they didn't have a few more days in Ottawa because a former NHL player had rallied nearly sixty current and former hockey stars who planned to fly in on February 20 to play shinny with the truckers and host a party from the stage to drum up support.

Lich said she wished the convoy put out its manifesto earlier, but otherwise had no misgivings. "I would do it all over again in a second," she said.

On March 5, Pawlak and Dichter published a "concluding" press release touting the convoy's achievements, from lifting of provincial restrictions to lawsuits against the Emergencies Act to more general shifts the political climate (several candidates in the ongoing Conservative leadership race have been competing to prove who supported the convoy better and who supported it first).

Wrote Pawlak and Dichter: "We are very grateful to the truckers and volunteers who made this demonstration possible. Without their sacrifice, the public's voice would continue to be silenced. The Freedom Convoy has inspired people around the world to stand up and make their voices heard against senseless government tyranny enabled through the sowing of fear and division. Thanks to them, the government can now hear us loud and clear."

CONCLUSION

For all that convoy organizers talk about their accomplishments and achievements in their three weeks in Ottawa, there's an elephant in the room. The federal government didn't lift a single of its vaccine mandates or COVID restrictions. By the end of the convoy, public sector workers still had to be vaccinated to work. Quarantine rules were still dependent on vaccination status. The unvaccinated were still barred from planes and trains. Even the vaccine mandate for cross-border truckers, which sparked the convoy idea in the minds of truckers Brigitte Belton and Chris Barber, remained. In the end, the federal government proved more stubborn than the convoy itself.

That does not mean the convoy was a failure. It claims credit for Erin O'Toole's ousting as Conservative leader and the expedited removal of several provinces' COVID restrictions, although these wins are relatively minor.

Its real success was far more unexpected. The movement united disparate groups that seldom see eye to eye in politics: French Canadians and alienated westerners, Indigenous people and suburban Ontarians, libertarians and social conservatives. This took place under the banner of freedom, ignoring the conventional left-right political divide. The convoy coalition reminded me of that old Ronald Reagan line about how an 80 percent ally isn't a 20 percent enemy.

The protesters found strength in their numbers, which were large enough to disprove Justin Trudeau's "fringe minority" label. By remaining peaceful until the very end, the convoy rose above the attacks from the media and the government, and proved them all wrong. Short of outright capitulation from the federal government, which was always an unlikely goal, the convoy was only ever going to end through force or with protesters getting bored and going home on their own. It took three weeks for the force to come, but it did.

The convoy also revealed a class fault line in Canadian politics and media. People were incredulous that a group of blue-collar truckers could bring a G-7 capital to its knees for three weeks. Even those who hated the convoy were baffled that Justin Trudeau and the City of Ottawa didn't seem to have any way of dealing with it, which is why, near the end, counter protests were mounted on Ottawa streets. You might have found the convoy objectionable, but the government's response was embarrassing from the get-go.

In a roundabout way, the convoy's greatest contribution to the cause of freedom was revealing how far the state was prepared to go to stop those who seek it. First, they tried to dismiss them, then malign them, then cast them as violent insurrectionists. None of it stuck. In the absence of violence, the media clung to any isolated anecdote that could be used to undermine the convoy as a whole.

What fascinated me most about the convoy were those behind it. People with no leadership or organizational experience showed up and became key players in a rapidly growing organization created on a whim, and wound up supporting an even bigger and faster-growing movement. When I was in Ottawa and learned of the command centres, strategy meetings, media relations teams, IT departments, intelligence and counterintelligence desks, and yes, the catering office, I knew there was a story unfolding that needed to be told. The paradox is that for all the sophistication I describe, Freedom Corp and the convoy organizers had no real authority over anyone but themselves.

They admit as much. Organizers were generally quite proud to tell me that each protester—each trucker—was his or her own leader and could decide what to do, how to behave, and when to go. This was what made the convoy such a risky exercise, but also what made it all the more impressive when the predicted violence never turned up. The truckers grew to trust the organizers—the high-profile ones getting the media attention, and the quiet ghosts who did a lot of heavy-lifting but never wanted glory or recognition.

Of the dozens of people I approached for this book, nearly everyone was happy to speak. Many of them had hours and hours of stories to tell from this crazy time in Ottawa, which was as defining in their own lives as it was for the country. The convoy showed that a moment chooses its leaders more than leaders choose their moment. When Canada was ready for a fight for freedom, a scrappy group of truckers and their friends was there to make it. It started with a honk.

NOTES

1 Cosmin Dzsurdzsa, "Trudeau calls convoy a 'small fringe minority' who hold 'unacceptable views,'" True North, January 26, 2022, https://tnc.news/2022/01/26/trudeau-calls-convoy-a-small-fringe-minority-who-hold-unacceptable-views/.

2 Marie Oakes, "Parliament Today deletes tweet suggesting donations to convoy could be providing 'financial services' for 'terrorist activity,'" Westphalian Times, January 27, 2022, https://tnc.news/2022/01/30/the-canadian-legacy-medias-ten-worst-spins-on-the-truckersforfreedom-convoy/.

3 Emma Colton, "Canadian news host slammed for suggesting Russia behind massive 'freedom' trucker protest," FoxNews.com, January 30, 2022, https://www.foxnews.com/world/cbc-canada-russia-freedom-convoy-vaccine-protest-criticisms.

4 Brigitte Belton [gidget_642], "#Windsor #cbsa #threats #gastqpo," TikTok, November 17, 2021, https://www.tiktok.com/@gidget_642/video/7031587574389034287.

5 Public Health Agency of Canada," Government of Canada announces adjustments to Canada's border measures," November 19, 2021, https://www.canada.ca/en/public-health/news/2021/11/government-of-canada-announces-adjustments-to-canadas-border-measures.html.

6 Grace Kay, "US to require truckers crossing US border be fully vaccinated, starting in January," Business Insider, November 23, 2021, https://www.businessinsider.com/truckers-vaccine-mandate-drivers-crossing-us-border-biden-2021-11.

7 Government of Canada, "COVID-19 Vaccination in Canada," https://health-infobase.canada.ca/covid-19/vaccination-coverage/.

8 Canadian Trucking Alliance, "US-Canada vaccine proposals for truckers need rethinking to soften economic, supply chain pain," news release, November 19, 2021, https://www.globenewswire.com/news-release/2021/11/19/2338457/0/en/CTA-US-Canada-Vaccine-Proposals-for-Truckers-Need-Rethinking-to-Soften-Economic-Supply-Chain-Pain.html.

9 Cece M. Scott, "Freedoms Collide. Freedoms Divide," *City Life, March 15, 2022, https://mycitylife.ca/people/special-feature/freedom-convoy-truckers-ottawa-canada/*.

10 Steve Scherer, "Canada drops vaccine mandate for its truckers after pressure from industry," Reuters, January 13, 2022, https://www.reuters.com/world/americas/canadian-truckers-stay-exempt-covid-19-vaccine-requirements-2022-01-13/.

11 Public Health Agency of Canada, "Requirements for truckers entering Canada in effect as of January 15, 2022," Statement from Jean-Yves Duclos, Omar Alghabra, and Marco Mendicino, January 13, 2022, https://www.canada.ca/en/public-health/news/2022/01/requirements-for-truckers-entering-canada-in-effect-as-of-january-15-2022.html.

12 Brigitte Belton [gidget_642], Convoy update, TikTok, January 15, 2022, https://www.tiktok.com/@gidget_642/video/7053313101080530223.

13 9News, "Queensland truckie convoy heads for NSW to protest mandatory vaccine," August 30, 2021, https://www.9news.com.au/national/coronavirus-queensland-nsw-truck-drivers-protest-against-mandatory-covid-19-vaccine-for-essential-workers/76330fce-f6ea-4c89-a22e-1b9ccd31c03a.

14 James Bauder, post to Facebook in Canada Unity, August 30, 2021, https://www.facebook.com/groups/CanadaUnity/posts/931657194359200.

15 Dave Dormer, "United We Roll convoy '100%' successful, says organizer despite concerns over funds raised," CBC News, February 23, 2019, https://www.cbc.ca/news/canada/calgary/alberta-united-we-roll-convoy-organizer-1.5031454.

16 Canada Unity, Facebook post, December 30, 2021, https://www.facebook.com/CanadaUnity/posts/3000388900291586.

17 Pat King, "QUICK UPDATE," The Real Pat King on Facebook, January 12, 2022, https://www.facebook.com/therealpatking/videos/405809597896484.

18 Pat King, "Convoy Update: Convoy Organizers Join In," The Real Pat King on Facebook, January 13, 2022, https://www.facebook.com/therealpatking/videos/373761267850240.

19 Gillian Findlay, "Convoy Organizer Pat King answers questions on racist videos, 'catch a bullet' comment," The Fifth Estate, CBC, February 26, 2022, https://www.youtube.com/watch?v=96XjD2NkOUc.

20 Chris Barber [@bigred19755], TikTok video, January 20, 2022, https://www.tiktok.com/@bigred19755/video/7055506179514010886.

21 Freedom Convoy 2022, Facebook video, January 23, 2022, https://www. facebook.com/watch/live/?ref=watch_permalink&v=397538718792789.

22 *Tucker Carlson Tonight*, "An Orwellian vaccine registry could be coming to the US, says Canadian trucker," Fox News, January 28, 2022, https://video. foxnews.com/v/6294064548001#sp=show-clips.

23 Alex McKeen, "Three 'Freedom Convoy' organizers pull back the curtain on the hopes, tension and infighting that marked the occupation," *Toronto Star*, March 26, 2022, https://www.thestar.com/news/canada/2022/03/26/ three-key-freedom-convoy-organizers-pull-back-the-curtain-on-the-hopes-tension-and-infighting-that-marked-their-protest.html.

24 CBC News, "Truckers protest dangerous conditions on B.C. highways," January 22, 2022, https://www.cbc.ca/news/canada/british-columbia/ truckers-rally-bc-highway-conditions-1.6324447.

25 Reid Small, "BC truckers to join convoy across Canada in protest of mandatory vaccine," *Western Standard*, January 17, 2022, https://westernstandardonline. com/2022/01/bc-truckers-to-join-convoy-across-canada-in-protest-of-mandatory-vaccine.

26 Courtney Greenberg, "Cross-country truckers convoy departs B.C. for Ottawa to protest vaccine mandate," *National Post*, January 22, 2022, https:// nationalpost.com/news/canada/cross-country-truckers-convoy-departs-b-c-for-ottawa-to-protest-vaccine-mandate.

27 Paul Johnson, "'Freedom convoy' of truckers opposing vaccine mandate leaves Metro Vancouver for Ottawa," Global News, January 23, 2022, https://globalnews. ca/video/8533296/freedom-convoy-of-truckers-opposing-vaccine-mandate-leaves-metro-vancouver-for-ottawa.

28 Bernadette Mullen, "Freedom Convoy: Truckers protesting Covid mandates travel to Ottawa," Discover Weyburn, January 19, 2022, https://discoverweyburn. com/articles/freedom-convoy--truckers-protesting-covid-mandates-travel-to-ottawa.

29 Canadian Trucking Alliance, "Canadian Trucking Alliance Statement on Road/ Border Protests," January 19, 2022, https://cantruck.ca/canadian-trucking-alliance-statement-on-road-border-protests/.

30 Canadian Trucking Alliance, "Canadian Trucking Alliance Statement to Those Engaged in Road/Border Protests, January 22, 2022, https://cantruck.ca/canadian-trucking-alliance-statement-to-those-engaged-in-road-border-protests/.

31 Roberto Wakerell-Cruz, "Canadian Trucking Alliance president donated to Liberals in 2018," The Post Millennial, January 26, 2022, https://thepostmillennial.com/canadian-trucking-alliance-president-donated-to-liberals-in-2018.

32 Omar Alghabra, Seamus O'Regan, Carla Qualtrough and Stephen Laskowski, "Joint Statement by Ministers Alghabra, O'Regan and Qualtrough, and the President of the Canadian Trucking Alliance," Government of Canada, January 25, 2022, https://www.canada.ca/en/transport-canada/news/2022/01/declaration-commune-des-ministresalghabra-oregan-et-qualtrough-et-du-president-de-lalliance-canadienne-du-camionnage.html.

33 Dan Ferguson, "Alberta-based Maverick party denies involvement in fund raising for 'freedom convoy,'" Castlegar News, January 24, 2022, https://www.castlegarnews.com/news/alberta-based-maverick-party-denies-involvement-in-fund-raising-for-freedom-convoy/.

34 James Menzies, "The murky matter of protests and the donations that drive them," TruckNews.com, January 21, 2022, https://www.trucknews.com/blogs/the-murky-matter-of-protests-and-the-donations-that-drive-them/.

35 Gerald Butts, Twitter post, January 22, 2022, https://twitter.com/gmbutts/status/1484916848848220170.

36 Canadian Anti-Hate Network, "The 'Freedom Convoy' is nothing but a vehicle for the far right," January 27, 2022, https://www.antihate.ca/the_freedom_convoy_is_nothing_but_a_vehicle_for_the_far_right

37 Alex Boutilier and Rachel Gilmore, "Far-right groups hope trucker protest will be Canada's 'January 6,'" Global News, January 25, 2022, https://globalnews.ca/news/8537433/far-right-groups-trucker-protest-jan-6/.

38 Rachel Gilmore, "Some trucker convoy organizers have history of white nationalism, racism," Global News, January 29, 2022, https://globalnews.ca/news/8543281/covid-trucker-convoy-organizers-hate/.

39 Grant LaFleche, "'Freedom Convoy' leader shared symbol od far-right hate group on TikTok," Toronto Star, January 28, 2022, https://www.thestar.com/news/canada/2022/01/28/freedom-convoy-leader-shared-symbol-of-far-right-hate-group-on-tiktok.html.

40 Alex Cooke, "Nova Scotia extends blockade ban to all roads, streets and highways," Global News, February 4, 2022, https://globalnews.ca/news/8596492/ns-blockade-ban-all-roads-streets-highways/.

Notes

41 Cosmin Dzsurdzsa, "Trudeau calls convoy a 'small fringe minority' who hold 'unacceptable views,'" True North, January 26, 2022, https://tnc. news/2022/01/26/trudeau-calls-convoy-a-small-fringe-minority-who-hold-unacceptable-views/.

42 Justin Trudeau, Twitter post, March 31, 2020, https://twitter.com/JustinTrudeau/ status/1245139169934016517.

43 Erin O'Toole, "It's time for solutions, and it's time for Canadians to come together," Toronto Sun, January 26, 2022, https://torontosun.com/opinion/columnists/ otoole-its-time-for-solutions-and-its-for-canadians-to-come-together.

44 City of Ottawa Media Availability, January 26, 2022, https://www.youtube. com/watch?v=uTf1EDjsu8E.

45 Ottawa Police Service Media Availability, January 28, 2022, https://www. youtube.com/watch?v=SFYcJQP5P3Y.

46 Guy Quenneville, "Convoy protesters were expected to leave Ottawa during 1st week, city says," CBC News, March 26, 2022, https://www.cbc.ca/news/ canada/ottawa/ottawa-freedom-convoy-protest-mathieu-fleury-councillor-inquiry-city-response-1.6397758.

47 Judy Trinh, "How organizers with police and military expertise may be helping Ottawa convoy protest," CBC News, February 9, 2022, https://www. cbc.ca/news/canada/convoy-protesters-police-tactical-knowledge-1.6345854.

48 Ottawa Police Service, "Significant traffic disruptions expected this weekend due to demonstration," January 26, 2022, https://www.ottawapolice.ca/ Modules/News/index.aspx?keyword=&date=01/01/2022&page=2&newsId= 9d1c61b6-8569-4aec-8481-2f32b7f61780.

49 David Fraser, "Almost $8M in 'Freedom Convoy' donations still unaccounted for, documents show," CBC News, April 7, 2022, https://www.cbc.ca/news/ canada/ottawa/freedom-convoy-donations-1.6410105.

50 Nichola Saminather, "TD Bank freezes accounts that received money for Canada protests," Reuters, February 12, 2022, https://www.reuters.com/ world/americas/td-bank-freezes-two-accounts-that-received-funds-support-canada-protests-2022-02-12/.

51 Health Canada, "Ivermectin not authorized to prevent or treat COVID-19; may cause serious health problem," public advisory, October 19, 2021, https:// recalls-rappels.canada.ca/en/alert-recall/ivermectin-not-authorized-prevent-or-treat-covid-19-may-cause-serious-health-problems.

52 Mike Arsalides, "Former Georgian College instructor in Ottawa as spokesperson for Freedom Convoy," CTV News, February 9, 2022, https://barrie.ctvnews.ca/former-georgian-college-instructor-in-ottawa-as-spokesperson-for-freedom-convoy-1.5775106.

53 Mike Blanchfield and Jim Bronskill, "Federal ministers blast Ottawa protesters seeking to join opposition 'coalition,'" *Toronto Star*, February 8, 2022, https://www.thestar.com/politics/2022/02/08/feds-ottawa-mayor-meet-to-discuss-covid-19-protests-clogging-canadian-capital.html.

54 Mark Gollom, "Anger over defacement of Terry Fox statue a sign of his 'unique' legacy, says mayor of icon's hometown," CBC News, February 1, 2022, https://www.cbc.ca/news/canada/ottawa/terry-fox-statue-convoy-1.6333867.

55 Blacklock's Reporter, "Convoy Allegation Disproven," April 29, 2022, https://www.blacklocks.ca/convoy-allegation-disproven/.

56 Matias Muñoz, Twitter post, February 6, 2022, https://twitter.com/TiMunoz/status/1490473045965815812.

57 Ted Raymond, "Suspect charged in downtown Ottawa arson last month not connected with 'Freedom Convoy': police," CTV News, March 21, 2022, https://ottawa.ctvnews.ca/suspect-charged-in-downtown-ottawa-arson-last-month-not-connected-with-freedom-convoy-police-1.5828171.

58 Matias Muñoz, Twitter post, March 21, 2022, https://twitter.com/TiMunoz/status/1506012500671696905.

59 Shepherds of Good Hope, Twitter post, January 30, 2022, https://twitter.com/sghottawa/status/1487854425368633344.

60 @Backyardfarmer420, Twitter post, January 29, 2022, https://twitter.com/Backyardfarmer3/status/1487601494312509445.

61 Candice Malcolm, "Everything we know so far about the Nazi Flag guy," True North, January 30, 2022, https://tnc.news/2022/01/30/everything-we-know-so-far-about-the-nazi-flag-guy2/.

62 Emily Pasiuk, "Edmonton-area MP under fire for photo of him near flag bearing Nazi symbol," CBC News, January 30, 2022, https://www.cbc.ca/news/canada/edmonton/edmonton-area-mp-under-fire-for-photo-of-him-near-flag-bearing-nazi-symbol-1.6333266.

63 Cross Country Checkup, "Why the word 'freedom' has become such a rallying cry for protesters," CBC News, February 13, 2022, https://www.cbc.ca/radio/checkup/what-s-your-reaction-to-the-ottawa-standoff-and-the-

border-blockades-1.6349636/why-the-word-freedom-is-such-a-useful-rallying-cry-for-protesters-1.6349865.

64 Jonathan Bradley, "Antisemitic leaflet was a hate hoax pushed by legacy media and left-wing politicians," True North, February 7, 2022, https://tnc.news/2022/02/07/anti-semitic-leaflet-was-a-hate-hoax-pushed-by-legacy-media-and-left-wing-politicians/.

65 CBC News, "Protest convoy had 'worst display of Nazi propaganda in this country,' anti-hate advocate says," January 30, 2022, https://www.cbc.ca/player/play/1997828675918.

66 John Paul Tasker, "Trudeau accuses Conservative MPs of standing with 'people who wave swastikas,'" CBC News, February 17, 2022, https://www.cbc.ca/news/politics/trudeau-conservative-swastikas-1.6354970.

67 Toronto Sun, "Toronto MP thinks a Freedom Convoy term is call for Hitler," February 22, 2022, https://torontosun.com/news/national/toronto-mp-thinks-a-freedom-convoy-term-is-call-for-hitler.

68 Rupa Subramanya, "What the Truckers Want," Common Sense, February 10, 2022, https://bariweiss.substack.com/p/what-the-truckers-want.

69 Jordan Peterson, What the Truckers Do and Do Not Want, The Jordan B Peterson Podcast, February 15, 2022, https://www.youtube.com/watch?v=P8tzXazvyHQ.

70 Elon Musk, Twitter post, January 27, 2022, https://twitter.com/elonmusk/status/1486772334635536395.

71 Donald Trump Jr., "Heroic Truck Driver Stands Up To Medical Tyranny," January 25, 2022, https://www.facebook.com/watch/?ref=external&v=2712087222431976.

72 Jonathan Bradley, "Trump says Canadian truckers 'being hunted down like enemies of their own government,'" True North, February 27, 2022, https://tnc.news/2022/02/27/trump-says-canadian-truckers-being-hunted-down-like-enemies-of-their-own-government/.

73 Sergio Olmos, "US anti-vaccine mandate campaigns aim to mimic Canadian convoy tactic," The Guardian, February 4, 2022, https://www.theguardian.com/us-news/2022/feb/04/us-anti-vaccine-mandate-convoy-canada.

74 Annabelle Olivier, "COVID-19: Quebec premier drops plan to tax people who are unvaccinated," Global News, February 1, 2022, https://globalnews.ca/

news/8585595/covid-19-quebec-premier-drops-plan-to-tax-people-who-are-unvaccinated/.

75 Phil Heidenreich, "COVID-19: Kenney announces Alberta vaccine passport program ending at midnight," Global News, February 8, 2022, https://globalnews.ca/news/8603220/alberta-covid-19-restrictions-lifted-update-february-8/.

76 David Giles, "Saskatchewan moves to end all COVID-19 public health orders," Global News, February 8, 2022, https://globalnews.ca/news/8603376/saskatchewan-end-covid-19-public-health-orders/.

77 Joshua Freeman, "Doug Ford says plan in works to remove Ontario's vaccine passport system," CTV News, February 11, 2022, https://toronto.ctvnews.ca/doug-ford-says-plan-in-works-to-remove-ontario-s-vaccine-passport-system-1.5777857.

78 Freedom Convoy 2022, Facebook post,

79 Rachel Aiello, "MPs warned about security risks related to convoy, O'Toole plans to meet truckers," CTV News, January 27, 2022, https://www.ctvnews.ca/politics/mps-warned-about-security-risks-related-to-convoy-o-toole-plans-to-meet-truckers-1.5757134.

80 Candice Bergen, "Statement from Conservative Leader Candice Bergen on trucker protest," Twitter post, February 4, 2022, https://twitter.com/CandiceBergenMP/status/1489700789505376259.

81 Josh Aldrich, "'That's $44 million per day': Coutts border blockade hits Alberta economy and trade," Calgary Herald, February 2, 2022, https://calgaryherald.com/business/thats-44-million-per-day-coutts-border-blockade-slams-alberta-economy-and-trade.

82 Freedom Convoy 2022, "Freedom Convoy Statement," Facebook video, February 14, 2022, https://www.facebook.com/watch/?v=640216597247971.

83 Max Hartshorn, "The economic nightmare that wasn't? Border blockades had little effect on trade, data reveals," Global News, April 26, 2022, https://globalnews.ca/news/8770775/border-blockades-trade-impact-data/.

84 Amanda Connolly, "Conservatives' Candice Bergen urges trucker convoy: 'Take down the barricades,'" Global News, February 10, 2022, https://globalnews.ca/news/8609809/trucker-convoy-candice-bergen-conservatives/.

85 Lorrie Goldstein, "Federal intelligence expert says Freedom Convoy donors no threat," Toronto Sun, February 26, 2022, https://torontosun.com/opinion/columnists/goldstein-federal-intelligence-expert-says-freedom-convoy-donors-no-threat.

86 Jim Watson, Twitter post, February 4, 2022, https://twitter.com/jimwatson
ottawa/status/1489747604909039622.

87 GoFundMe, "GoFundMe Statement on the Freedom Convoy 2022 Fundraiser,"
Medium, February 4, 2022, https://medium.com/gofundme-stories/update-
gofundme-statement-on-the-freedom-convoy-2022-fundraiser-4ca7e9714e82.

88 GiveSendGo, Twitter post, February 10, 2022, https://twitter.com/
GiveSendGo/status/1491940399505682434.

89 Alec Schemmel, "Critics say Canadian state broadcaster is using illegally
hacked data to out convoy donors," CBS Austin, February 15, 2022, https://
cbsaustin.com/news/nation-world/critics-say-canadian-state-broadcaster-is-
using-illegally-hacked-data-to-out-convoy-donors.

90 Sammy Hudes, "PC Staffer fired over Freedom Convoy donation suing Ford,
journalists," Politics Today, May 5, 2022, https://www.politicstoday.news/
queens-park-today/pc-staffer-fired-over-freedom-convoy-donation-suing-ford-
journalists/.

91 Andrew Lupton, "Largest single Ontario convoy donation came from this
London, Ont., businessman," CBC News, February 16, 2022, https://www.cbc.
ca/news/canada/london/convoy-donations-london-businessman-1.6352450.

92 Randy Richmond, "$25K donation to Ottawa protest 'about freedom': London
businessman," London Free Press, February 16, 2022, https://lfpress.com/
news/local-news/25k-donation-to-ottawa-protest-about-freedom-londoner.

93 Andrew Lawton, "Legacy media's stories about convoy attendee don't add up,"
True North, March 30, 2022, https://tnc.news/2022/03/30/legacy-medias-
stories-about-convoy-attendee-dont-add-up/.

94 Ekin Genç, "The 'Freedom Convoy' Bitcoin Donations Have Been Frozen
and Seized," Vice, March 15, 2022, https://www.vice.com/en/article/jgmnpd/
the-freedom-convoy-bitcoin-donations-have-been-frozen-and-seized.

95 Josh Pringle and Ted Raymond, "Police target fuel supply for 'Freedom Convoy'
demonstration in Ottawa," CTV News, February 6, 2022, https://ottawa.
ctvnews.ca/police-target-fuel-supply-for-freedom-convoy-demonstration-in-
ottawa-1.5769811.

96 Joanne Chianello, "If policing can't end Ottawa's protest, then what can?"
CBC News, February 3, 2022, https://www.cbc.ca/news/canada/ottawa/
policing-end-ottawa-protest-covid-19-mandates-1.6337563.

97 Jon Willing, "Chief Sloly: We need 1,800 more cops and civilians to handle crisis,"

Ottawa Citizen, February 8, 2022, https://ottawacitizen.com/news/local-news/chief-sloly-we-need-1800-more-cops-and-civilians-to-handle-crisis.

98 Ryan Tumilty, "Ottawa mayor calls for feds to provide 1,800 more police to clear protesters," Saltwire, February 7, 2022, https://www.saltwire.com/atlantic-canada/news/ottawa-mayor-calls-for-feds-to-provide-1800-more-police-to-clear-protesters-100690157/.

99 Dean French, "Why I negotiated with the truckers in Ottawa," *National Post*, February 17, 2022, https://nationalpost.com/opinion/dean-french-why-i-negotiated-with-the-truckers-in-ottawa.

100 Benjamin Dichter, Twitter post, February 13, 2022, https://twitter.com/BJdichter/status/1493033482355838976.

101 Chris Barber [@bigred19755], TikTok video, February 14, 2022, https://www.tiktok.com/@bigred19755/video/7064627488462474502.

102 Laura Osman, "RCMP cleared border blockades without Emergencies Act powers, committee hears," The Canadian Press, May 10, 2022, https://ottawa.citynews.ca/national-news/rcmp-cleared-border-blockades-without-emergencies-act-powers-committee-hears-5354395.

103 Rachel Gilmore, "Trudeau says Emergencies Act won't override fundamental rights — but experts aren't so sure," Global News, February 15, 2022, https://globalnews.ca/news/8621256/freedom-convoy-emergencies-act-trudeau-charter-rights/

104 Adam Toy, "4 charged with conspiracy to murder after raid on Coutts blockade," Global News, February 15, 2022, https://globalnews.ca/news/8622765/conspiracy-to-murder-weapons-chargers-coutts-blockade-raid/.

105 Justin Ling, "Ottawa protests: 'strong ties' between some ocupiers and far-right extremists, minister says," *The Guardian*, February 16, 2022, https://www.theguardian.com/world/2022/feb/16/ottawa-blockade-strong-ties-extremists.

106 Jeremy MacKenzie, Untitled video, Diagolon, n.d., https://diagolon.org/.

107 Ottawa Police Service, "A further notice to demonstrators," February 16, 2022, https://www.ottawapolice.ca/en/news-and-community/weekend-demonstration-information-and-updates.aspx#A-further-Notice-to-Demonstrators-February-16-2022.

108 Maggie Parkhill, "Who is who? A guide to the major players in the trucker convoy protest," CTV News, February 10, 2022, https://www.ctvnews.ca/

canada/who-is-who-a-guide-to-the-major-players-in-the-trucker-convoy-protest-1.5776441.

109 Rachel Emmanuel, "More Canadians strongly oppose Emergencies Act: Mainstreet poll," iPolitics, February 19, 2022, https://ipolitics.ca/news/more-canadians-strongly-oppose-emergencies-act-mainstreet-poll.

110 Paul Champ, Twitter post, February 17, 2022, https://twitter.com/paulchamplaw/status/1494477818184536068.

111 Jagmeet Singh, "Jagmeet Singh Speech on Emergencies Act," NDP, February 17, 2022, https://www.ndp.ca/news/jagmeet-singh-speech-emergencies-act.

112 Nathaniel Erskine-Smith, "Speech on the Emergencies Act," February 21, 2022, https://beynate.ca/speech-on-the-emergencies-act/.

113 Canadian Civil Liberties Association, "CCLA will fight invocation of Emergencies Act in court," February 17, 2022, https://ccla.org/major-cases-reports/ccla-will-fight-invocation-of-emergencies-act-in-court-2/.

114 Canadian Constitution Foundation, "Emergencies act challenge," February 17, 2022, https://theccf.ca/?case=emergencies-act-challenge.

115 Andrew Lawton, "Alberta takes Trudeau to court over use of Emergencies Act," True North, May 7, 2022, https://tnc.news/2022/05/07/alberta-takes-trudeau-to-court-over-use-of-emergencies-act/.

116 Sara Frizzell and Shaamini Yogaretnam, "Convoy protest organizers Tamara Lich, Chris Barber, Pat King arrested in Ottawa," CBC News, February 17, 2022, https://www.cbc.ca/news/canada/ottawa/tamara-lich-chris-barber-arrested-ottawa-1.6355960.

117 Benjamin Dichter, Twitter post, February 18, 2022, https://twitter.com/BJdichter/status/1494780866681319427.

118 Cheryl Gallant, "Conservative MPs support protest," interview with Benita Pedersen, Facebook, February 8, 2022, https://www.facebook.com/watch/?v=1797757053753209.

119 Ottawa Police Service, Twitter post, February 18, 2022, https://twitter.com/ottawapolice/status/1494806139971813376.

120 Ottawa Police Service, Twitter post, February 18, 2022, https://twitter.com/ottawapolice/status/1494683910411751426?lang=en.

121 New York Times, Twitter post, February 19, 2022, https://twitter.com/nytimes/status/1495072626607280131.

122 David Paisley, "The Last Stand. Live from the Freedom Convoy in Ottawa,

Canada," *Live from the Shed*, February 19, 2022, https://www.youtube.com/watch?v=Q2K2Gt3nM0Q&t=1500s.

123 Melissa Lantsman, Twitter post, February 20, 2022, https://twitter.com/MelissaLantsman/status/1495450824620875776.

124 Ottawa Police Service, Twitter post, February 20, 2022, https://twitter.com/ottawapolice/status/1495367658132361216.

125 Peter Zimonjic, "Most bank accounts frozen under the Emergencies Act are being released, committee hears," CBC News, February 22, 2022, https://www.cbc.ca/news/politics/emergency-bank-measures-finance-committee-1.6360769.

126 Michael Woods, "'Freedom Convoy' donations frozen, could flow to Ottawa residents," CTV News, February 28, 2022, https://ottawa.ctvnews.ca/freedom-convoy-donations-frozen-could-flow-to-ottawa-residents-1.5799105.

127 Erika Ibrahim, "GiveSendGo tells court it is refunding convoy donations amid freezing order," The Canadian Press, March 9, 2022, https://globalnews.ca/news/8671685/give-send-go-donation-refunds/.

128 David Fraser, "Almost $8M of 'Freedom Convoy' donations still unaccounted for, documents show," CBC News, April 7, 2022, https://globalnews.ca/news/8671685/give-send-go-donation-refunds/.

129 Prime Minister's Office, "Prime Minister announces Public Order Emergency Commission following the invocation of the Emergencies Act," April 25, 2022, https://pm.gc.ca/en/news/news-releases/2022/04/25/prime-minister-announces-public-order-emergency-commission-following.

ABOUT THE AUTHOR

Andrew Lawton is a senior journalist at True North and host of The Andrew Lawton Show. He previously hosted a daily talk show on Global News Radio. He has published written work across the world, including in the Washington Post, the National Post, the Toronto Sun, and on Global News. Andrew has appeared as a commentator on CBC, CTV, TVO, CTS, and on BBC World.